College Culture, Student Success

DEBRA J. ANDERSON
Bristol Community College

OTHER TITLES IN THE LONGMAN TOPICS READER SERIES

A Longman Topics Reader

College Culture, Student Success

DEBRA J. ANDERSON
Bristol Community College

PEARSON
Longman

New York   San Francisco   Boston
London   Toronto   Sydney   Tokyo   Singapore   Madrid
Mexico City   Munich   Paris   Cape Town   Hong Kong   Montreal

Acquisitions Editor: Lauren A. Finn
Senior Marketing Manager: Sandra McGuire
Senior Supplements Editor: Donna Campion
Production Manager: Stacey Kulig
Project Coordination, Text Design, and Electronic Page Makeup:
    Katie Fuller, S4Carlisle Publishing Services
Cover Design Manager: Wendy Ann Fredericks
Cover Photo: © Ross Anderson/CORBIS. All Rights Reserved.
Senior Manufacturing Buyer: Dennis J. Para
Printer and Binder: Edwards Brothers Malloy
Cover Printer: Edwards Brother Malloy

For permission to use copyrighted material, grateful acknowledgment is made to the copyright holders on pp. 193–196, which are hereby made part of this copyright page.

Library of Congress Cataloging-in-Publication Data

Anderson, Debra J. (Debra Jean), 1969-
  College culture, student success/Debra J. Anderson.
    p. cm.
  ISBN-13: 978-0-321-43305-3
  ISBN-10: 0-321-48641-2
  1. Education, Higher—Social aspects—United States.
    2. Educational sociology—United States. I. Title.

  LC191.94.A46 2008
  378.1'98--dc22

                                    2007038272

Please visit us at www.ablongman.com

ISBN 13: 978-0-321-43305-3
ISBN 10: 0-321-43305-X

14—V069—15 14 13

To my son, Nicholas Ara:
May you always be as open-hearted and curious as you are today.

CONTENTS

Rhetorical Contents

PREFACE FOR INSTRUCTORS

College Culture, Student Success is a reader for first-year students from diverse backgrounds who are in college for a variety of reasons and at a variety of junctures in their lives. These students may be traditional-age learners, international students, nontraditional learners, parents, grandparents, distance learners, or first-generation college students. They are also likely to be lifelong learners taking one course, gifted high school students in dual enrollment programs, people for whom English is a second language, students with learning or physical disabilities, or professionals transitioning from one career to another. The one thing they all have in common, however, is that their lives will intersect, and they will all contribute to and draw from the culture of college.

This book is designed to help students find an entry point into this sometimes intimidating and often exciting culture by providing selections by and about successful students who face a range of academic and personal challenges in higher education, as well as selections about issues relevant to today's college students, such as distance learning, online communities, service learning, time management, plagiarism, and life outside the classroom.

Though some faculty will adopt this book as the only required text for their first-year writing or first-year seminar course, others may find that it serves as an appropriate complement to another text. For example, in a first-year writing or reading course, the instructor may want to pair this book with a text that explains rhetorical strategies, critical reading, and/or research techniques in detail. Because *College Culture, Student Success* includes a collection of exemplary professional and student writing that employs these strategies and techniques as well as pre- and postreading questions, students can use this book to apply the critical thinking and composition skills they are learning in the course's primary text. In either case, the flexibility of this book will enhance what is happening in the class without overshadowing the instructor's curriculum.

A READER THAT REFLECTS STUDENTS' FIRST-YEAR EXPERIENCES

College Culture, Student Success is designed to help students develop reading, writing, and thinking skills as well as help them become familiar with the common customs, underlying assumptions, and strategies for success associated with being a college student. The book is organized to reflect the experiences that first-year college students typically face in chronological order.

- Chapter One, "I Wasn't Brought Up That Way: Where Home Culture Meets College Culture," asks students to compare their experiences with others who have dared to take the step away from home cultures toward the culture of college.
- Chapter Two, "A Day in the Life: Opportunities and Challenges In and Out of the Classroom," looks at how life outside of the classroom can impact one's success as a student and citizen. Challenges such as balancing work and school, managing relationships, and negotiating "the party scene" are explored.
- Chapter Three, "Who's in Charge Here? Exploring Self-Awareness and Personal Responsibility," aims at inspiring students to think about the role that they play in determining their own destiny. There is an emphasis on self-advocacy and problem-solving skills when confronting issues as varied as learning disabilities, family responsibilities, and procrastination.
- Chapter Four, "Learning and Unlearning: Reinventing Yourself as a Learner," invites students to examine the skills of successful learners as they consider their own learning styles, academic strengths, and shortcomings to move toward a better understanding of themselves and the demands of college.
- Chapter Five, "Becoming an Educated Person: Intellectual Curiosity, Integrity, and Critical Thinking in College and Beyond," helps students consider questions about the value of their education. Further, it informs students about some of the challenges and opportunities that await them as educated and ambitious people.

PREREADING QUESTIONS, QUESTIONS FOR WRITING AND DISCUSSION, AND WEBSITES

Through the **Making It Matter** questions that precede each selection, students will search their own backgrounds for what they know about topics to create a context for what they are about to learn in the reading.

Also preceding each reading is one **Breaking It Down** question that asks students to consider how rhetorical modes and/or specific techniques are employed in the piece. Here students will have an opportunity to apply their understanding of composition and rhetorical concepts to real-world writing.

The **Questions for Writing and Discussion** provide an opportunity for students to think critically about what they have read and how it relates to them as college students. These questions allow students to explore and practice different rhetorical and research techniques as they apply to topics in the readings.

The **Making Connections** questions at the end of each chapter encourage students to draw on themes and opposing perspectives presented in the selections. By comparing and contrasting rhetorical approaches and points of view, students will wrestle with diverse ideas and strategies as they practice their analytical skills.

Finally, in the **Exploring the Web** section at the end of each chapter, students will have the opportunity to delve deeper into issues and encounter the most current perspectives by following these annotated links. Instructors may use these links to give students a starting point for research assignments, expose them to useful resources, or provide interactive practice with academic skill development.

College Culture, Student Success is an affordable, pedagogically flexible reader built around a theme that students can relate to as they embark on their college journey. In addition to introducing this diverse group of students to college culture, it also aims at inspiring intellectual curiosity and improving critical thinking, writing, and reading abilities.

ACKNOWLEDGMENTS

I'd like to thank the reviewers who commented on an early draft of *College Culture, Student Success*. They are

Maggie McLaughlin - Olympic College;
Randall McClure - Minnesota State University - Mankato;
Dottie Burkhart - Davidson County Community College;
Sheila Stewart - South Suburban College;
Caroline Mains - Palo Alto College;
Patricia Allen - Cape Cod Community College;
Sean Nighbert - St. Philip's College;
Doug Rigby - Lehigh Carbon Community College.

I appreciate your thoughtful responses and suggestions. I'd also like to thank my editor, Lauren Finn, who suggested I propose this book and ably shepherded it through the publication process. Your insights, patience, and understanding meant a great deal to me. Additionally, I'd like to acknowledge production manager Stacey Kulig, production editor Katie L. Fuller, copyeditor Kirsten Balayti, editor assistants Bristol Maryott and Carmen O'Donnell, and intern Jenny Mitchell. Thank you for your fine work.

Thanks also go to my colleagues and friends—Joseph Salvatore, New School University; John Brown, Shawsheen Regional Vocational Technical High School; and Sandra Lygren, Elizabeth Kemper French, and J. Thomas Grady, Bristol Community College—all of whom provided me with advice and support. William J. Kelly, also of Bristol Community College, deserves special thanks for mentoring me through every stage of this project.

My deepest gratitude goes to my parents, Patricia and the late Ara Deroian, whose sacrifices provided my brother Steve and me with the opportunity to become college students. They also taught us to appreciate and enjoy our time in college. During those years, we earned degrees, began important friendships and learned enough about ourselves and the world to pursue satisfying careers. Without these experiences, this book could not have been written.

Finally, I am indebted to my husband, Eric, whose love, encouragement, and sense of humor make anything seem possible.

DEBRA J. ANDERSON

Deciding to go to college is an important step for anyone. For some, it was always the plan, something your parents, teachers, co-curricular activities, and jobs have been preparing you for. For others, college is the last place you thought you'd end up, assuming that once you walked off that stage at high school graduation you had completed all the formal education you'd ever need. But somehow, you came to desire something that this college experience could offer you. Or perhaps you're in college after a long break from education, looking for a career change or simply pursing an area of interest that you never had the opportunity to pursue before. Regardless of why you made this decision, you are a member of a new community, a subculture known as "college students."

Like all cultures, this culture of college has its own *language*, or at least its own vocabulary. Words like *syllabus, semester, midterms, service learning,* and many others (some unique to your school) will become a part of your everyday conversations.

College culture also has its own behavioral *norms*. Political activism, all-nighters, study groups, and tailgate parties are likely to be far more common in your life than in the lives of those who are part of other American subcultures.

Finally, as a college student, you will be part of a culture that shares *values*. These values may include such things as academic integrity, friendship, intellectual curiosity, and a sense of responsibility for the world we live in.

You will make an impact on the culture in your classrooms, dorms, and clubs, and therefore on college culture as a whole. Undoubtedly, the culture will also affect you. In fact, being a part of this college culture may change and challenge you in ways you didn't anticipate.

College Culture, Student Success was written with you and the journey you will be taking as a college student in mind. One goal of this text is to help you become knowledgeable about the culture and larger community that you are joining, to give you some perspective on this journey from those who have been—or are still going—through it. You may find this text unique in a few ways:

- It is brief and more affordable than many of the books you'll be buying this semester.
- It includes readings by not only professional writers (a pediatrician, a computer programmer, a famous civil rights leader, and an Iranian expatriate are among them) but also fellow college students from public, private, and community colleges.
- It is designed to help you apply and explore the critical reading and writing skills you are learning in general education courses.
- The reading selections will give you a variety of perspectives about issues you are confronting as a college student, such as balancing work and school; the party scene; the role of the Internet in your academic, personal, and professional life; academic integrity; and negotiating with friends and family as your evolving identity as a college student takes shape.
- In the **Exploring the Web** sections that end each chapter, you will find additional resources for such things as applying for scholarships, finding online communities, and learning study and time management skills.

In short, I hope that the voices presented in this book speak to you and your experience, but my greater hope is that this book provides opportunities for you to develop your own voice.

DEBRA J. ANDERSON

I Wasn't Brought Up That Way: Where Home Culture Meets College Culture

Overview

As discussed in "Preface for Students," coming to college means participating in and belonging to a culture with its own set of norms, values, and behaviors. And even though you are likely coming to college with an open mind, it's important to remember that you were not born into this culture. You were born into a particular ethnic, urban, rural, or suburban socioeconomic group, and the culture of this group may or may not integrate smoothly with college culture. But your life is where these two worlds meet. How you respond to the conflicts and challenges that these two cultures present may be one of the ways that you define yourself long after your college days are over.

This chapter asks you to consider the diverse paths that have led people to college, and the cultures those paths wind themselves through before they end at the door of a college or university admissions office. As you read these selections, think about your own path and your life before college. To what extent will you embrace and preserve the culture you were born into? To what extent will you open yourself to change?

MAKING IT MATTER

What are your first memories of going to school? Did you feel shy and unsure about this new world or did you feel comfortable and happy? Consider the new world of college. Does being part of a

1

college community change or expand your perspective on the other communities you are also a part of?

BREAKING IT DOWN

Essays that compare or contrast typically use a point-by-point or block structure. The point-by-point structure develops each supporting paragraph around a particular point of comparison, whereas the block structure creates a fuller picture of one topic and follows it with a well-developed view of the topic it is being compared with or contrasted against. As you read, try to discern which structure Suina uses and consider why this choice best serves his purpose and audience.

And Then I Went to School
JOSEPH H. SUINA

Joseph H. Suina is Professor of Education emeritus at the University of New Mexico and a member of the tribal council of the Cochiti Pueblo. This selection was originally published in his book Linguistic and Cultural Influences on Learning Mathematics.

───────────── ✦ ─────────────

I lived with my grandmother from the ages of five through nine. It was the early 1950s when electricity had not yet invaded the homes of the Cochiti Indians. The village day school and health clinic were first to have it and to the unsuspecting Cochitis this was the approach of a new era in their uncomplicated lives.

Transportation was simple then. Two good horses and a sturdy wagon met most needs of a villager. Only five or six individuals possessed an automobile in the Pueblo of 300. A flatbed truck fixed with wooden rails and a canvas top made a regular Saturday trip to Santa Fe. It was always loaded beyond capacity with Cochitis taking their wares to town for a few staples. With an escort of a dozen barking dogs, the straining truck made a noisy exit, northbound from the village.

During those years, Grandmother and I lived beside the plaza in a one-room house. It consisted of a traditional fireplace, a makeshift cabinet for our few tin cups and dishes, and a wooden crate that held our two buckets of all-purpose water. At the far end of the room were two rolls of bedding we used as comfortable sitting "couches." Consisting of thick quilts, sheepskin, and assorted blankets, these bed rolls were undone each night. A wooden pole the length of one side of the room was suspended about 10 inches from the ceiling beams. A modest collection of colorful shawls, blankets, and sashes was draped over the pole making this part of the room most interesting. In one corner was a bulky metal trunk for our ceremonial wear and a few valuables. A dresser, which was traded for some of my grandmother's well-known pottery, held the few articles of clothing we owned and the "goody bag." Grandmother always had a flour sack filled with candy, store bought cookies, and Fig Newtons. These were saturated with a sharp odor of moth balls. Nevertheless, they made a fine snack with coffee before we turned in for the night. Tucked securely in my blankets, I listened to one of her stories or accounts of how it was when she was a little girl. These accounts seemed so old fashioned compared to the way we lived. Sometimes she softly sang a song from a ceremony. In this way I fell asleep each night.

Earlier in the evening we would make our way to a relative's house if someone had not already come to visit us. I would play with the children while the adults caught up on all the latest. Ten-cent comic books were finding their way into the Pueblo homes. For us children, these were the first link to the world beyond the Pueblo. We enjoyed looking at them and role playing as one of the heroes rounding up the villains. Everyone preferred being a cowboy rather than an Indian because cowboys were always victorious. Sometimes, stories were related to both children and adults. These get-togethers were highlighted by refreshments of coffee and sweet bread or fruit pies baked in the outdoor oven. Winter months would most likely include roasted pinon nuts or dried deer meat for all to share. These evening gatherings and sense of closeness diminished as the radios and televisions increased over the following years. It was never to be the same again.

The winter months are among my fondest recollections. A warm fire crackled and danced brightly in the fireplace and the aroma of delicious stew filled our one-room house. To me the house was just right. The thick adobe walls wrapped around the two of us protectingly during the long freezing nights.

Grandmother's affection completed the warmth and security I will always remember.

Being the only child at Grandmother's, I had lots of attention and plenty of reasons to feel good about myself. As a pre-schooler, I already had the chores of chopping firewood and hauling in fresh water each day. After "heavy work," I would run to her and flex what I was certain were my gigantic biceps. Grandmother would state that at the rate I was going I would soon attain the status of a man like the adult males in the village. Her shower of praises made me feel like the Indian Superman of all times. At age five, I suppose I was as close to that concept of myself as anyone.

In spite of her many years, Grandmother was still active in the village ceremonial setting. She was a member of an important women's society and attended all the functions, taking me along to many of them. I would wear one of my colorful shirts she handmade for just such occasions. Grandmother taught me the appropriate behavior at these events. Through modeling she taught me to pray properly. Barefooted, I would greet the sun each morning with a handful of cornmeal. At night I would look to the stars in wonderment and let a prayer slip through my lips. I learned to appreciate cooperation in nature and my fellowmen early in life. About food and material things, Grandmother would say, "There is enough for everyone to share and it all comes from above, my child." I felt very much a part of the world and our way of life. I knew I had a place in it and I felt good about me.

At age six, like the rest of the Cochiti six-year-olds that year, I had to begin my schooling. It was a new and bewildering experience. One I will not forget. The strange surroundings, new concepts about time and expectations, and a foreign tongue were overwhelming to us beginners. It took some effort to return the second day and many times thereafter.

To begin with, unlike my grandmother, the teacher did not have pretty brown skin and a colorful dress. She was not plump and friendly. Her clothes were one color and drab. Her pale and skinny form made me worry that she was very ill. I thought that explained why she did not have time just for me and the disappointed looks and orders she seemed to always direct my way. I didn't think she was so smart because she couldn't understand my language. "Surely that was why we had to leave our 'Indian' at home." But then I did not feel so bright either. All I could say in her language was "yes teacher," "my name is Joseph Henry," and "when is lunch time." The teacher's odor took some getting used to also. In fact, many times it made me sick right before lunch. Later, I learned from the girls that this odor was something she wore called perfume.

The classroom too had its odd characteristics. It was terribly huge and smelled of medicine like the village clinic I feared so much. The walls and ceiling were artificial and uncaring. They were too far from me and I felt naked. The fluorescent light tubes were eerie and blinked suspiciously above me. This was quite a contrast to the fire and sunlight that my eyes were accustomed to. I thought maybe the lighting did not seem right because it was man-made, and it was not natural. Our confinement to rows of desks was another unnatural demand from our active little bodies. We had to sit at these hard things for what seemed like forever before relief (recess) came midway through the morning and afternoon. Running carefree in the village and fields was but a sweet memory of days gone by. We all went home for lunch because we lived within walking distance of the school. It took coaxing and sometimes bribing to get me to return and complete the remainder of the school day.

School was a painful experience during those early years. The English language and the new set of values caused me much anxiety and embarrassment. I could not comprehend everything that was happening but yet I could understand very well when I messed up or was not doing so well. The negative aspect was communicated too effectively and I became unsure of myself more and more. How I wished I could understand other things just as well in school.

The value conflict was not only in school performance but in other areas of my life as well. For example, many of us students had a problem with head lice due to "the lack of sanitary conditions in our homes." Consequently, we received a severe shampooing that was rough on both the scalp and the ego. Cleanliness was crucial and a washing of this type indicated to the class how filthy a home setting we came from. I recall that after one such treatment I was humiliated before my peers with a statement that I had "She'na" (lice) so tough that I must have been born with them. Needless to say, my Super Indian self-image was no longer intact.

My language, too, was questionable from the beginning of my school career. "Leave your Indian (language) at home" was like a trademark of school. Speaking it accidentally or otherwise was a sure reprimand in the form of a dirty look or a whack with a ruler. This punishment was for speaking the language of my people which meant so much to me. It was the language of my grandmother and I spoke it well. With it, I sang beautiful songs and prayed from my heart. At that young and tender age, comprehending why I had to part with it was most difficult for me. And yet at home I was encouraged to attend school so that I might have a better life in the future. I knew I had a good village life already but this was communicated less and less each day I was in school. . . .

I had to leave my beloved village of Cochiti for my education beyond Grade 6. I left to attend a Bureau of Indian Affairs boarding school 30 miles from home. Shined shoes and pressed shirt and pants were the order of the day. I managed to adjust to this just as I had to most of the things the school shoved at me or took away from me. Adjusting to leaving home and the village was tough indeed. It seemed the older I got, the further away I became from the ways I was so much a part of. Because my parents did not own an automobile, I saw them only once a month when they came up in the community truck. They never failed to come supplied with "eats" for me. I enjoyed the outdoor oven bread, dried meat, and tamales they usually brought. It took a while to get accustomed to the diet of the school. I longed for my grandmother and my younger brothers and sisters. I longed for my house. I longed to take part in a Buffalo Dance. I longed to be free.

I came home for the four-day Thanksgiving break. At first, home did not feel right anymore. It was much too small and stuffy. The lack of running water and bathroom facilities were too inconvenient. Everything got dusty so quickly and hardly anyone spoke English. I did not realize I was beginning to take on the white man's ways, the ways that belittled my own. However, it did not take long to "get back with it." Once I established my relationships with family, relatives, and friends I knew I was where I came from and where I belonged.

Leaving for the boarding school the following Sunday evening was one of the saddest events in my entire life. Although I enjoyed myself immensely the last few days, I realized then that life would never be the same again. I could not turn back the time just as I could not do away with school and the ways of the white man. They were here to stay and would creep more and more into my life. The effort to make sense of both worlds together was painful and I had no choice but to do so. The schools, television, automobiles, and other white man's ways and values had chipped away at the simple cooperative life I grew up in. The people of Cochiti were changing. The winter evening gatherings, exchanging of stories, and even the performing of certain ceremonies were already only a memory that someone commented about now and then. Still the demands of both worlds were there. The white man's was flashy, less personal, but comfortable. The Indian was both attracted and pushed toward these new ways that he had little to say about. There was no choice left but to compete with the white man on his terms for survival. For that I knew I had to give up a part of my life.

Determined not to cry, I left for school that dreadfully lonely night. My right hand clutched tightly the mound of cornmeal Grandmother placed there and my left hand brushed away a tear as I made my way back to school.

Questions for Writing and Discussion

1. Suina writes that he was encouraged to attend school so that he "might have a better life in the future." What changes does he note about his life as a result of going to school? To what degree, if any, does his life get better in the course of the essay? In what ways do you think attending college will provide you with a better life? What, if anything, will you be giving up?

2. Suina states that when children were role playing comic book stories "everyone preferred to be a cowboy rather than an Indian because cowboys were always victorious." Can you think of any images you came in contact with as a child that stereotyped a particular group? To what extent did these images affect your view of yourself or others?

3. Despite the fact that Suina's native language is not English, his teacher requires him to speak English at school. Do you think this was in the best interest of Suina, and is in the best interest of other children who live in the United States but do not speak English at home? Do some research on bilingualism and English-only education and take a position on this controversial issue. State clearly why you feel that one approach is superior to the other.

4. Suina discusses the "values conflict" between his life at home and his life at school. Have you ever experienced a values conflict in your own life because you were living in two worlds? Describe one situation in which you became aware of this conflict. How did you cope with it?

5. Compare the culture of college with the culture of another environment you have been in. It could be your high school or another school you have attended, a place you have worked, or another community you have been a member of. What do you see as the differences between the two cultures? Do you feel more comfortable in one culture than the other? Why or why not?

6. While Suina seemed to enjoy his life in the Pueblo, he came to appreciate it even more once he was required to spend much of his time away from home at boarding school. Discuss a situation in which you came to more fully appreciate something about your life as the result of a new experience.

MAKING IT MATTER

Think about the way that you communicate in the course of a day. You may speak to friends, family, coworkers, employers, children, teachers, classmates, and others. Consider the differences in the ways you speak to each of these people. Did you learn to modify the way you communicate with different people, or did it come naturally?

BREAKING IT DOWN

Amy Tan compares the different "Englishes" that she uses to make a point about the power of language. As you read, construct the thesis that Tan is implying through her comparison.

Mother Tongue
AMY TAN

Amy Tan grew up in California and earned degrees from San Jose State University. She is best known for her novel Joy Luck Club *(1989), which was also adapted for film. "Mother Tongue" first appeared in a literary magazine called the* Threepenny Review.

---◆---

I am not a scholar of English or literature. I cannot give you much more than personal opinions on the English language and its variations in this country or others.

I am a writer. And by that definition, I am someone who has always loved language. I am fascinated by language in daily life. I spend a great deal of my time thinking about the power of language—the way it can evoke an emotion, a visual image, a complex idea, or a simple truth. Language is the tool of my trade. And I use them all—all the Englishes I grew up with.

Recently, I was made keenly aware of the different Englishes I do use. I was giving a talk to a large group of people, the same talk I had already given to half a dozen other groups. The nature of the talk was about my writing, my life, and my book, *The Joy Luck Club*. The talk was going along well enough, until I remembered one major difference that made the whole talk sound wrong. My mother was in the room. And it was perhaps the first time she had heard me give a lengthy speech, using the kind of English I have never used with her. I was saying things like, "The intersection of memory upon imagination" and "There is an aspect of my fiction that relates to thus-and-thus"—a speech filled with carefully wrought grammatical phrases, burdened, it suddenly seemed to me, with nominalized forms, past perfect tenses, conditional phrases, all the forms of standard English that I had learned in school and through books, the forms of English I did not use at home with my mother.

Just last week, I was walking down the street with my mother, and I again found myself conscious of the English I was using, the English I do use with her. We were talking about the price of new and used furniture and I heard myself saying this: "Not waste money that way." My husband was with us as well, and he didn't notice any switch in my English. And then I realized why. It's because over the twenty years we've been together I've often used that same kind of English with him, and sometimes he even uses it with me. It has become our language of intimacy, a different sort of English that relates to family talk, the language I grew up with.

So you'll have some idea of what this family talk I heard sounds like, I'll quote what my mother said during a recent conversation which I videotaped and then transcribed. During this conversation, my mother was talking about a political gangster in Shanghai who had the same last name as her family's, Du, and how the gangster in his early years wanted to be adopted by her family, which was rich by comparison. Later, the gangster became more powerful, far richer than my mother's family, and one day showed up at my mother's wedding to pay his respects. Here's what she said in part:

"Du Yusong having business like fruit stand. Like off the street kind. He is Du like Du Zong—but not Tsung-ming Island people. The local people call putong, the river east side, he belong to that side local people. That man want to ask Du Zong father take him in like become own family. Du Zong father wasn't look down on him, but didn't take seriously, until that man big like become a mafia. Now important person, very hard to inviting him. Chinese way, came only to show respect, don't stay for dinner. Respect for making big celebration, he shows up. Mean gives lots of respect. Chinese custom. Chinese social life that way. If too important won't have to stay too long. He come to my wedding. I didn't see, I heard it. I gone to boy's side, they have YMCA dinner. Chinese age I was nineteen."

You should know that my mother's expressive command of English belies how much she actually understands. She reads the *Forbes* report, listens to *Wall Street Week,* converses daily with her stockbroker, reads all of Shirley MacLaine's books with ease—all kinds of things I can't begin to understand. Yet some of my friends tell me they understand 50 percent of what my mother says. Some say they understand 80 to 90 percent. Some say they understand none of it, as if she were speaking pure Chinese. But to me, my mother's English is perfectly clear, perfectly natural. It's my mother tongue. Her language, as I hear it, is vivid, direct, full of observation and imagery. That was the language that helped shape the way I saw things, expressed things, made sense of the world.

Lately, I've been giving more thought to the kind of English my mother speaks. Like others, I have described it to people as "broken" or "fractured" English. But I wince when I say that. It has always bothered me that I can think of no way to describe it other than "broken," as if it were damaged and needed to be fixed, as if it lacked a certain wholeness and soundness. I've heard other terms used, "limited English," for example. But they seem just as bad, as if everything is limited, including people's percep- tions of the limited English speaker.

I know this for a fact, because when I was growing up, my mother's "limited" English limited *my* perception of her. I was ashamed of her English. I believed that her English reflected the quality of what she had to say. That is, because she expressed them imperfectly her thoughts were imperfect. And I had plenty of empirical evidence to support me: the fact that people in department stores, at banks, and at restaurants did not take her seriously, did not give her good service, pretended not to understand her, or even acted as if they did not hear her.

My mother has long realized the limitations of her English as well. When I was fifteen, she used to have me call people on the phone to pretend I was she. In this guise, I was forced to ask for information or even to complain and yell at people who had been rude to her. One time it was a call to her stockbroker in New York. She had cashed out her small portfolio and it just so happened we were going to go to New York the next week, our very first trip outside California. I had to get on the phone and say in an adolescent voice that was not very convincing, "This is Mrs. Tan."

And my mother was standing in the back whispering loudly, "Why he don't send me check, already two weeks late. So mad he lie to me, losing me money."

And then I said in perfect English, "Yes, I'm getting rather concerned. You had agreed to send the check two weeks ago, but it hasn't arrived."

Then she began to talk more loudly. "What he want, I come to New York tell him front of his boss, you cheating me?" And I was trying to calm her down, make her be quiet, while telling the stockbroker, "I can't tolerate any more excuses. If I don't receive the check immediately, I am going to have to speak to your manager when I'm in New York next week." And sure enough, the following week there we were in front of this astonished stockbroker, and I was sitting there red-faced and quiet, and my mother, the real Mrs. Tan, was shouting at his boss in her impeccable broken English.

We used a similar routine just five days ago, for a situation that was far less humorous. My mother had gone to the hospital for an appointment, to find out about a benign brain tumor a CAT scan had revealed a month ago. She said she had spoken very good English, her best English, no mistakes. Still, she said, the hospital did not apologize when they said they had lost the CAT scan and she had come for nothing. She said they did not seem to have any sympathy when she told them she was anxious to know the exact diagnosis, since her husband and son had both died of brain tumors. She said they would not give her any more information until the next time and she would have to make another appointment for that. So she said she would not leave until the doctor called her daughter. She wouldn't budge. And when the doctor finally called her daughter, me, who spoke in perfect English—lo and behold—we had assurances the CAT scan would be found, promises that a conference call on Monday would be held, and apologies for any suffering my mother had gone through for a most regrettable mistake.

I think my mother's English almost had an effect on limiting my possibilities in life as well. Sociologists and linguists probably will tell you that a person's developing language skills are more influenced by peers. But I do think that the language spoken in the family, especially in immigrant families which are more insular, plays a large role in shaping the language of the child. And I believe that it affected my results on achievement tests, I.Q. tests, and the SAT. While my English skills were never judged as poor, compared to math, English could not be considered my strong suit. In grade school I did moderately well, getting perhaps B's, sometimes B-pluses, in English and scoring perhaps in the sixtieth or seventieth percentile on achievement tests. But those scores were not good enough to override my opinion that my true abilities lay in math and science, because in those areas I achieved A's and scored in the ninetieth percentile or higher.

This was understandable. Math is precise; there is only one correct answer. Whereas, for me at least, the answers on English tests were always a judgment call, a matter of opinion and personal experience. Those tests were constructed around items like fill-in-the-blank sentence completion, such as, "Even though Tom was ____, Mary thought he was ____." And the correct answer always seemed to be the most bland combinations of thoughts, for example, "Even though Tom was shy, Mary thought he was charming," with the grammatical structure "even though" limiting the correct answer to some sort of semantic opposites, so you wouldn't get answers like, "Even though Tom was foolish, Mary thought he was ridiculous." Well, according to my mother, there were very few limitations as to what Tom could have been and what Mary might have thought of him. So I never did well on tests like that.

The same was true with word analogies, pairs of words in which you were supposed to find some sort of logical, semantic relationship—for example, "*Sunset* is to *nightfall* as ____ is to ____." And here you would be presented with a list of four possible pairs, one of which showed the same kind of relationship: *red* is to *stoplight, bus* is to *arrival, chills* is to *fever, yawn* is to *boring.* Well, I could never think that way. I knew what the tests were asking, but I could not block out of my mind the images already created by the first pair, "*sunset* is to *nightfall*"—and I would see a burst of colors against a darkening sky, the moon rising, the lowering of a curtain of stars. And all the other pairs of words—red, bus, stoplight, boring—just threw up a mass of confusing images, making it impossible for me to sort out something as logical as saying: "A sunset precedes nightfall" is the same as "a chill precedes a fever." The only way I would have gotten that answer right would have been to imagine an associative situation, for example, my being disobedient and staying out past sunset, catching a chill at night, which turns into feverish pneumonia as punishment, which indeed did happen to me.

I have been thinking about all this lately, about my mother's English, about achievement tests. Because lately I've been asked, as a writer, why there are not more Asian Americans represented in American literature. Why are there few Asian Americans enrolled in creative writing programs? Why do so many Chinese students go into engineering? Well, these are broad sociological questions I can't begin to answer. But I have noticed in surveys—in fact, just last week—that Asian students, as a whole, always do significantly better on math achievement tests than in English. And this makes me think that there are other Asian-American students whose English spoken in the home might also be described as "broken" or "limited." And perhaps they also have teachers who are steering them away from writing and into math and science, which is what happened to me.

Fortunately, I happen to be rebellious in nature and enjoy the challenge of disproving assumptions made about me. I became an English major my first year in college, after being enrolled as pre-med. I started writing non-fiction as a freelancer the week after I was told by my former boss that writing was my worst skill and I should hone my talents toward account management.

But it wasn't until 1985 that I finally began to write fiction. And at first I wrote using what I thought to be wittily crafted sentences, sentences that would finally prove I had mastery over the English language. Here's an example from the first draft of a story that later made its way into *The Joy Luck Club,* but without this line: "That was my mental quandary in its nascent state." A terrible line, which I can barely pronounce.

Fortunately, for reasons I won't get into today, I later decided I should envision a reader for the stories I would write. And the reader I decided upon was my mother, because these were stories about mothers. So with this reader in mind—and in fact she did read my early drafts—I began to write stories using all the Englishes I grew up with: the English I spoke to my mother, which for lack of a better term might be described as "simple"; the English she used with me, which for lack of a better term might be described as "broken"; my translation of her Chinese, which could certainly be described as "watered down"; and what I imagined to be her translation of her Chinese if she could speak in perfect English, her internal language, and for that I sought to preserve the essence, but neither an English nor a Chinese structure. I wanted to capture what language ability tests can never reveal: her intent, her passion, her imagery, the rhythms of her speech and the nature of her thoughts.

Apart from what any critic had to say about my writing, I knew I had succeeded where it counted when my mother finished reading my book and gave me her verdict: "So easy to read."

Questions for Writing and Discussion

1. Tan writes that she became "keenly aware of the different Englishes" when her mother was in an audience of academics with whom she typically used "standard forms of English." Have you ever been in a situation in which the way you were speaking or writing made you feel awkward or inauthentic in some way? Describe the situation and why you felt as you did. What, if anything, did you do to cope?

2. Tan suggests that questions for standardized tests can imply certain cultural assumptions. Do some research on cultural bias associated with nationally normed or standardized tests such as the SAT, PSAT, ACT, or Miller Analogies. Based on your experience with any of these tests and your research, do you think that cultural bias is a controversial issue worthy of discussion? What is your position on this issue?

3. Do you believe, as Tan does, that the way that people speak affects our perceptions about that person's skills or abilities? Have you ever been involved in a situation in which someone was stereotyped because of the way he or she communicated? Describe the situation and explain what you took away from the experience.

4. Write a short letter or email to your best friend about one aspect of your experience as a college student. Write a letter to your instructor that covers the same topic. Then adapt the letter into a short article for your college or university newspaper. Assume this article will be part of a special edition designed for new students at orientation. Analyze the difference between the language and style of the three pieces of writing. What do those differences tell you about your relationship with each of your audiences and how you want to be perceived by those audiences?

MAKING IT MATTER

Do your parents or other family members have dreams for you? Are your dreams consistent with theirs, or is there a conflict between what you see as a "good life" and what they imagine for you?

BREAKING IT DOWN

As you read, consider the way that Lubrano integrates description, dialogue, figurative language, and scholarship from experts to tell his story. How do these techniques enhance the effectiveness of his narrative?

Bricklayer's Boy
ALFRED LUBRANO

Alfred Lubrano is a columnist for the Philadelphia Inquirer *and a commentator for National Public Radio's "Weekend Edition". He is the author of* Limbo: Blue Collar Roots, White Collar Dreams *(2003), which explores his experience and those of other white-collar professionals who, like himself, grew up in working-class families. "Bricklayer's Boy" first appeared in* Gentlemen's Quarterly *in 1989.*

———————— ✦ ————————

My father and I were college buddies back in the mid 1970s. While I was in class at Columbia, struggling with the esoterica du jour, he was on a bricklayer's scaffold not far up the street, working on a campus building.

Sometimes we'd hook up on the subway going home, he with his tools, I with my books. We didn't chat much about what went on during the day. My father wasn't interested in Dante, I wasn't up on arches. We'd share a *New York Post* and talk about the Mets.

My dad has built lots of places in New York City he can't get into: colleges, condos, office towers. He makes his living on the outside. Once the walls are up, a place takes on a different feel for him, as if he's not welcome anymore. It doesn't bother him, though. For my father, earning the dough that paid for my entrée into a fancy, bricked-in institution was satisfaction enough, a vicarious access.

We didn't know it then, but those days were the start of a branching off, a redefining of what it means to be a workingman in our family. Related by blood, we're separated by class, my father and I. Being the white-collar son of a blue-collar man means being the hinge on the door between two ways of life.

It's not so smooth jumping from Italian old-world style to U.S. yuppie in a single generation. Despite the myth of mobility in America, the true rule, experts say, is rags to rags, riches to riches. According to Bucknell University economist and author Charles Sackrey, maybe 10 percent climb from the working to the professional class. My father has had a tough time accepting my decision to become a mere newspaper reporter, a field that pays just a little more than construction does. He wonders why I haven't cashed in on that multi-brick education and taken on some lawyer-lucrative job. After bricklaying for thirty years, my father promised himself I'd never pile bricks and blocks into walls for a living. He figured an education—genielike and benevolent— would somehow rocket me into the consecrated trajectory of the upwardly mobile, and load some serious loot into my pockets. What he didn't count on was his eldest son breaking blue-collar rule No. 1: Make as much money as you can, to pay for as good a life as you can get.

He'd tell me about it when I was nineteen, my collar already fading to white. I was the college boy who handed him the wrong wrench on help-around-the-house Saturdays. "You better make a lot of money," my blue-collar handy dad wryly warned me as we huddled in front of a disassembled dishwasher I had neither the inclination nor the aptitude to fix. "You're gonna need to hire someone to hammer a nail into a wall for you."

In 1980, after college and graduate school, I was offered my first job, on a now-dead daily paper in Columbus, Ohio. I broke the news in the kitchen, where all the family business is discussed. My mother wept as if it were Vietnam. My father had a few questions: "Ohio? Where the hell is Ohio?"

I said it's somewhere west of New York City, that it was like Pennsylvania, only more so. I told him I wanted to write, and these were the only people who'd take me.

"Why can't you get a good job that pays something, like in advertising in the city, and write on the side?"

"Advertising is lying," I said, smug and sanctimonious, ever the unctuous undergraduate. "I wanna tell the truth."

"The truth?" the old man exploded, his face reddening as it does when he's up twenty stories in high wind. "What's truth?" I said it's real life, and writing about it would make me happy. "You're happy with your family," my father said, spilling blue-collar rule No. 2. "That's what makes you happy. After that, it all comes down to dollars and cents. What gives you comfort besides your family? Money, only money."

During the two weeks before I moved, he reminded me that newspaper journalism is a dying field, and I could do better. Then he pressed advertising again, though neither of us knew anything about it, except that you could work in Manhattan, the borough with the water-beading high gloss, the island polished clean by money. I couldn't explain myself, so I packed, unpopular and confused. No longer was I the good son who studied hard and fumbled endearingly with tools. I was hacking people off

One night, though, my father brought home some heavy tape and that clear, plastic bubble stuff you pack your mother's second-string dishes in. "You probably couldn't do this right," my father said to me before he sealed the boxes and helped me take them to UPS. "This is what he wants," my father told my mother the day I left for Columbus in my grandfather's eleven-year-old gray Cadillac "What are you gonna do?" After I said my goodbyes, my father took me aside and pressed five $100 bills into my hands. "It's okay," he said over my weak protests. "Don't tell your mother."

When I broke the news about what the paper was paying me, my father suggested I get a part-time job to augment the income. "Maybe you could drive a cab." Once, after I was chewed out by the city editor for something trivial, I made the mistake of telling my father during a visit home. "They pay you nothin', and they push you around too much in that business," he told me, the rage building. "Next time, you gotta grab the guy by the throat and tell him he's a big jerk."

"Dad, I can't talk to the boss like that."

"Tell him. You get results that way. Never take any shit." A few years before, a guy didn't like the retaining wall my father and his partner had built. They tore it down and did it again, but the guy still bitched. My father's partner shoved the guy into the freshly laid bricks. "Pay me off," my father said, and he and his partner took the money and walked. Blue-collar guys have no patience for office politics and corporate bile-swallowing. Just pay me off and I'm gone. Eventually, I moved on to a job in Cleveland, on a paper my father has heard of. I think he looks on it as a sign of progress, because he hasn't mentioned advertising for a while.

When he was my age, my father was already dug in with a trade, a wife, two sons and a house in a neighborhood in Brooklyn not far from where he was born. His workaday, family-centered life has been very much in step with his immigrant father's. I sublet what the real-estate people call a junior one-bedroom in a dormlike condo in a Cleveland suburb. Unmarried and unconnected in an insouciant, perpetual student kind of way, I rent movies during the week and feed single women in restaurants on Saturday nights. My dad asks me about my dates, but he goes crazy over the word "woman." "A girl," he corrects. "You went out with a girl. Don't say 'woman.' It sounds like you're takin' out your grandmother."

I've often believed blue-collaring is the more genuine of lives, in greater proximity to primordial manhood. My father is provider and protector, concerned only with the basics: food and home, love and progeny. He's also a generation closer to the heritage, a warmer spot nearer the fire that forged and defined us. Does heat dissipate and light fade further from the source? I live for my career, and frequently feel lost and codeless, devoid of the blue-collar rules my father grew up with. With no baby-boomer groomer to show me the way, I've been choreographing my own tentative shuffle across the wax-shined dance floor on the edge of the Great Middle Class, a different rhythm in a whole new ballroom.

I'm sure it's tough on my father, too, because I don't know much about bricklaying, either, except that it's hell on the body, a daily sacrifice. I idealized my dad as a kind of dawn-rising priest of labor, engaged in holy ritual. Up at five every day, my father has made a religion of responsibility. My younger brother, a Wall Street white-collar guy with the sense to make a decent salary, says he always felt safe when he heard Dad stir before him, as if Pop were taming the day for us. My father, fifty-five years old, but expected to put out as if he were three decades stronger, slips on machine-washable vestments of khaki cotton without waking my mother. He goes into the kitchen and turns on the radio to catch the temperature. Bricklayers have an occupational need to know the weather. And because I am my father's son, I can recite the five-day forecast at any given moment.

My father isn't crazy about this life. He wanted to be a singer and actor when he was young, but that was frivolous doodling to his Italian family, who expected money to be coming in, stoking the stove that kept hearth fires ablaze. Dreams simply were not energy-efficient. My dad learned a trade, as he was supposed to, and settled into a life of pre-scripted routing. He says he can't find the black-and-white publicity glossies he once had made.

Although I see my dad infrequently, my brother, who lives at home, is with the old man every day. Chris has a lot more blue-collar in him than I do, despite his management-level career; for a short time, he wanted to be a construction worker, but my parents persuaded him to go to Columbia. Once in a while he'll bag a lunch and, in a nice wool suit, meet my father at a construction site and share sandwiches of egg salad on semolina bread.

It was Chris who helped my dad most when my father tried to change his life several months ago. My dad wanted a civil-service bricklayer foreman's job that wouldn't be so physically demanding. There was a written test that included essay questions about construction work. My father hadn't done anything like it in forty years. Why the hell they needed bricklayers to write essays I have no idea, but my father sweated it out. Every morning before sunrise, Chris would be ironing a shirt, bleary-eyed, and my father would sit at the kitchen table and read aloud his practice essays on how to wash down a wall, or how to build a tricky corner. Chris would suggest words and approaches.

It was so hard for my dad. He had to take a Stanley Kaplan-like prep course in a junior high school three nights a week after work for six weeks. At class time, the outside men would come in, twenty-five construction workers squeezing themselves into little desks. Tough blue-collar guys armed with No. 2 pencils leaning over and scratching out their practice essays, cement in their hair, tar on their pants, their work boots too big and clumsy to fit under the desks.

"Is this what finals felt like?" my father would ask me on the phone when I pitched in to help long-distance. "Were you always this nervous?" I told him yes. I told him writing's always difficult. He thanked Chris and me for the coaching, for putting him through school this time. My father thinks he did okay, but he's still awaiting the test results. In the meantime, he takes life the blue-collar way, one brick at a time.

When we see each other these days, my father still asks how the money is. Sometimes he reads my stories; usually he likes them, although he recently criticized one piece as being a bit sentimental: "Too schmaltzy," he said. Some psychologists say that the blue-white-collar gap between fathers and sons leads to alienation, but I tend to agree with Dr. Al Baraff, a clinical psychologist and director of the Men-Center in Washington, D.C. "The core of the relationship is based on emotional and hereditary traits," Baraff says. "Class [distinctions] just get added on. If it's a healthful relationship from when you're a kid, there's a respect back and forth that'll continue."

Nice of the doctor to explain, but I suppose I already knew that. Whatever is between my father and me, whatever keeps us talking and keeps us close, has nothing to do with work and economic class.

During one of my visits to Brooklyn not long ago, he and I were in the car, on our way to buy toiletries, one of my father's weekly routines. "You know, you're not as successful as you could be," he began, blue-collar blunt as usual. "You paid your dues in school. You deserve better restaurants, better clothes." Here we go, I thought, the same old stuff. I'm sure every family has five or six similar big issues that are replayed like well-worn videotapes. I wanted to fast-forward this thing when we stopped at a red light.

Just then my father turned to me, solemn and intense. His knees were aching and his back muscles were throbbing in clockable intervals that registered in his eyes. It was the end of a week of lifting fifty-pound blocks. "I envy you," he said quietly. "For a man to do something he likes and get paid for it—that's fantastic." He smiled at me before the light changed, and we drove on. To thank him for the understanding, I sprang for the deodorant and shampoo. For once, my father let me pay.

Questions for Writing and Discussion

1. What is the significance of Lubrano's final sentence: "For once, my father let me pay"? Discuss a time in which you or someone you know took an action that may have seemed unremarkable to an outsider, but actually had a deeper, more symbolic meaning to those involved.

2. Lubrano explains that his father was satisfied with "vicarious access" to Columbia and other white-collar institutions because his sons were allowed into that world. Describe a situation in which your experience gave someone else "vicarious access" to that experience. How did you feel about sharing this experience? What impact did it have on the other person?

3. In describing his own experience, Lubrano touches on the "myth of mobility in America," explaining that the American Dream is more difficult and takes longer to attain than we might have been led to believe. How does your dream for your future compare to the traditional idea of the American Dream? How do you plan to attain your dream and overcome any obstacles you might encounter?

4. Much of Lubrano's essay illustrates the differences between blue-collar and white-collar culture. Which can you relate to most? Which do you respect and appreciate most? Do you place yourself in one of these two worlds or a combination? What are the advantages and disadvantages of your particular position?

5. Lubrano uses figurative language in his essay, such as "being the hinge on the door between two ways of life" (para. 4), "my collar already fading to white" (para. 6), and "I've been choreographing my own tentative shuffle across the wax-shined dance floor on the edge of the Great Middle Class, a different rhythm in a whole new ballroom" (para. 17). Use one of Lubrano's metaphors or figurative images, or a variation on one, as a title or starting point for your own essay about a related topic. If none of Lubrano's images fit your experience or thesis, create your own figurative image or metaphor that somehow relates to ideas in his essay.

MAKING IT MATTER

Think about jobs you've held or jobs you've seen family members hold. How do these jobs compare with work you do as a college student? Which is more challenging? Which is more rewarding? What do your answers to these questions tell you about your values?

BREAKING IT DOWN

As you read "The Meaning of Work," consider the ways in which Rodríguez helps his reader to construct a portrait of both himself and his father. How significant a role do sensory details and dialogue play in contributing to his point?

The Meaning of Work

RODRIGO JOSEPH RODRÍGUEZ

Rodrigo Joseph Rodríguez earned a master's degree in English from the University of Texas and a Ph.D. in curriculum and instruction at the University of Connecticut. This essay, originally entitled "'Here I Am': On Labor and the Everyday," was first published in Hispanic Magazine.

———————— ◆ ————————

Had you been born during my day, you would have known the meaning of work, my father says in Spanish. He looks at my hands and arms. "Had you not gone to college," Papi says, "you would be working." Perhaps I would have never boxed my books and said goodbye in the pursuit of academic success. Moreover, I would not spend so much time in libraries, universities, and museums. Instead, I would think of the more familiar life: marriage, family, a steady salary.

To Papi, after all, this was the dream that founded the United States, a country with immeasurable opportunity—the opportunities he rarely had, since he worked and lived in the shadows, speaking Spanish and following the cotton circuit. For Papi, doing work means doing physical labor, not sitting before a computer screen or curled up on the foldout La-Z-Boy with a book. It means using arm and muscle, putting your hands to everyday use.

Late in the evening, after we finished our homework and had our dinner, Papi would arrive from the refinery with dusty hair and an aching body. His lunchbox often held a treat for the first child who'd greet him as he entered the house. Work, work, work. He did not want his children to lead such a life. "If you study hard, you won't have to work like me," he'd warn us in Spanish. "Use this," he'd say, while pointing to his head. Then, he'd offer his hands and arms.

The only life he knew was that of a pipe fitter at the refinery in Pasadena, Texas. Before a holiday, a bonus from the refinery's payroll office usually awaited him. On such occasions, I looked forward to a father-and-son stroll. Once, while waiting in line, one of Papi's coworkers commented that I'd be a good worker when I grew older. "He'll work in air conditioning," my father retorted in English. "That's what you should have said," he later told me. At the age of eight, what did I know; what did *I* know?

Now that I am pursuing graduate study, I reflect on this academically privileged life, a life that has taken me throughout the United States and to other countries. Who would have thought? I wasn't always a bright student in high school. Every grading period, the Cs and Ds told me otherwise. I remember those who hardly believed in me.

It was an interior voice, a haunting voice that led me to the world of books. As a diligent student of letters, I read until my eyes squinted; I wrote until my arms ached. While still in high school, I remember sitting, looking out the windows of Houston's MTA buses, and wondering if I would ever receive my diploma to begin my university studies. I was not sure I could do it, but I did. This is not to say everything happened all at once, but I knew what I wanted: University Avenue—a foreign space. Maybe Papi's voice and Mami's hopes swirled in the back room of my brain. I like to think that everything was leading to this moment *now*.

In May 1997, my father attended my commencement in the rural quiet of Ohio, far away from our native Texas. I earned a bachelor's degree in English from Kenyon. And, here I am, as Abraham once said in the Bible, far from that time and place, yet so close. Soon, I will lead discussion in a class entitled "Masterworks of American Literature." I will ask my students, "What is *American* literature?" For the sake of hearing our nation's voices, I shall speak of American *literatures*. I shall raise my voice against the muffled noises of the air conditioner.

Unlike family members who entered through the back doors of public institutions in Texas, performing manual labor, I enter academic institutions through the front door. I am reminded of their spirit and physical labor, how they paved the way for me, one day, to open the pages of books they rarely had the time and, much less, the leisure to read.

Like the journeys of my forefathers and foremothers, who forged paths across borders, I must shape my space in the pursuit of academic success.

Questions for Writing and Discussion

1. Rodríguez's father wanted his son to "work in air conditioning," despite the fact that he himself was a pipe fitter. What does "working in air conditioning" imply about the type of work his father dreams of for his son? How does this dream relate to the comments that his father makes about "knowing the meaning of work"?

2. What do you value in a job or career—flexibility, fulfillment, a high salary, or something else? Has this always been your view, or has it changed as you've matured?

3. How does your definition of work compare to that of your parents or other family members? What do you think accounts for the similarities or differences?

4. In the final paragraph, Rodríguez pays tribute to his "forefathers and foremothers." Whom do you consider to be your forefathers and/or foremothers? To what degree are they responsible for your success? To what degree are they not responsible for it?

MAKING IT MATTER

Have differences of opinion about morality, religion, or politics created conflicts in your family or community? How do you cope with these conflicts? Is it always possible to be true to yourself and maintain your family or community bonds?

BREAKING IT DOWN

As you read this essay, ask yourself why Oliphant chooses to include anecdotes and specific examples of students who will benefit from the Point Foundation. Do these human stories make you more or less likely to support a program like this?

Abandoned but Not Alone
THOMAS OLIPHANT

Thomas Oliphant is an award-winning political correspondent and columnist for the Boston Globe, *where this selection was originally published.*

────────── ✦ ──────────

FORGET Alan Keyes—the right-wing tub-thumper, the talk-show noisemaker, the Republican pol, the conservative "Christian," the dad who abandoned his teenager because she happens to be gay.

The person to care about and take an interest in is Maya Keyes—the daughter, the young woman who got into Brown University, the kid who spent time teaching in India. Sadly, she is anything but a unique case of a budding scholar instantly impoverished by vindictive parents on the threshold of life.

On the brighter side, it turns out she is not alone, but in the embrace of an organization that was set up a few years ago to help in heart-breaking situations like hers. Thanks to The Point Foundation, she will make it to Brown after all. She will not only have financial aid, she will have at least one adult mentor to confide in as her undergraduate life unfolds.

She will have to work hard to keep her aid, too. She must maintain the equivalent of a 3.5 grade-point average and design a community service program for her "spare" time. Where higher education is concerned, that is as it should be. It's supposed to be hard, just not impossible because of cruel parents.

So will it go for 40 other young people honored a year ago with Point Foundation assistance. Vance Lancaster, the executive director, told me more than 1,000 teenagers applied for help last year, nearly 3,000 this year. What that means is, as he put it, "Maya Keyes is . . . only the tip of an iceberg, especially when you realize that we are unable to do all that much outreach to kids nationally." The foundation was established by a group of people who as students 30 years ago had also faced parental abandonment because they happened to be gay. They persevered, made it, and then made it big, resolving that they would use some of their wealth to provide the help they lacked. That what happened is still happening is a reminder that the fundamental sources of big-otry remain strong.

At the foundation, there's a story behind nearly every kid they help. One of the most poignant involves a freshman at Boston University, who is from Kentucky. Rummaging through his stuff one day, his father found a diary that disclosed his son's then-secret. When the young man returned home, he was led upstairs to his room, shown a packed suitcase, told his relatives had been contacted to make sure he was shunned, and then kicked out of the house by the father.

After being taken in by kind souls in his community, there was an attempt at partial reconciliation at home, which ended abruptly when the kid's parents cut off his Internet access after they discovered his contacts with the foundation.

Lancaster, who encounters this kind of heartbreak on almost every application, said there are cases of kids being rejected when they sought loans and scholarships in their communities, includ-ing young people who were National Merit scholars and gradua-tion valedictorians.

Reconciliation with initially cruel behavior by parents is something the foundation tries its best to encourage, but it is never easy. Lancaster mentioned one case—of a freshman at UCLA who is only 16 because he skipped two grades as a child—where the very process of applying to the foundation had given the family a topic to discuss, even though the topic of the kid's very identity was too raw.

The intense pain and anguish of these rejected kids is one reason the Point people are so determined to go beyond merely providing financial assistance. If needed, they provide an adult to be there on the first day of college, so that one of the more joyous rites of passage (the unloading of the car at the dormi-tory) doesn't take place in solitude. In the summer, there are retreats to expose students to career opportunities and to suc-cessful adults.

The idea is to combat the forces of marginalization that face young people trying to cope with sexual and gender identity. The societal forces are ugly enough; it is unspeakable that they would include so many parents.

The good news in the Keyes story is that the real grown-up in the family is going to have her chance. The tougher news is that only 40 such young people can currently be assisted. The foundation (www.thepointfoundation.org) has an active board, as well as an anonymous angel who underwrites its administrative and fund-raising costs. Every buck donated goes directly to help a young person.

The idea is not to undermine parents; it is to keep parents from undermining their kids' future.

Questions for Writing and Discussion

1. Oliphant takes a strong position against Alan Keyes and some of the other parents whom he accuses of "parental abandonment because [their children] happen to be gay." Do you think Oliphant's argument is reasonable? Why or why not?

2. The Point Foundation puts an emphasis on students having a mentor. Discuss a situation in your life when you relied on someone who acted like a mentor to help you achieve or cope with something. Based on this experience, what kind of support do you think a mentor could provide to you as a college student?

3. Everyone who receives assistance through the Point Foundation must design a community service project. If you were required to design a service project for your community, what would you do? What is the rationale for your project, and how would you go about making it a reality?

4. The Point Foundation is just one of a number of funding sources that the majority of college students don't know is available. Do some research on scholarships, loans, and grants and find at least one that you are eligible for. Write an article that provides other students like you with information about this opportunity for financial assistance.

MAKING IT MATTER

To what degree do you feel that the culture or environment you were raised in is still with you as you integrate into the culture of your college? Do you see this as a benefit or liability?

BREAKING IT DOWN

As you read, consider the point of view of this selection. How does this point of view enhance the reader's understanding of Larry Wakefield's dilemma?

Let the Colors Run

RON SUSKIND

Ron Suskind is a Washington, D.C.–based author and Pulitzer Prize–winning reporter. This excerpt is taken from A Hope in the Unseen: An American Odyssey from the Inner City to the Ivy League *(1998). This book follows the struggles of Cedric Jennings, an honors student growing up in inner-city Washington, D.C., who attends Brown University.*

✦

Larry Wakeford stares in silence at the blonde, butch-cut, mischievously cocked head of a student—a delightfully contentious senior named Leslie—and notices a ray of late afternoon sunlight reflecting off her nostril stud. He chuckles.

"Listen, Leslie, I'm not sure if I'm actually exercising some sort of tyranny or not. I'm just giving guidelines for an assignment," he says while leaning forward, fingertips on the edge of the seminar table, in a purposeful pose. "I think we need some sort of rubric, some sort of accepted criteria for our work in this class . . . or there would be chaos. We all can agree on at least that, can't we?"

Murmurs ripple across the room, a lovely, high-ceilinged address on the second floor of stately Sayles Hall, with dark wood paneling, aged to perfection, narrow twelve-foot windows, and twenty students in Fieldwork and Seminar in High School Education who are just limbering up.

The issue du jour involves "rubrics," or how the format of an assignment can favor the strengths of some students and highlight the weaknesses of others or, in any event, how it can stifle creativity. The subject, discussed theoretically in previous classes, has circled around to delicious relevance on this early March Monday's discussion of the upcoming midterm paper. It is noted simply on the syllabus as "five pages, typed, double-spaced, on the topic of diversity in the classroom, using observations from each student's fieldwork."

Larry is certain of one thing: his winking suggestion that the syllabus line may just be a starting point, that the students may actually search for "some sort of criteria" that "we all can agree on" and have it stick, will mean a few minutes of edgy, vigorous discussion. He crosses his arms, leans his back against the chalkboard, and lets them have at it, winning a respite, after an hour of lecturing, to watch how various kids might connect educational theory to their passionately held views about grading and fairness.

"Why couldn't we, for instance, write a three-act play that deals with issues of diversity in the class we're observing," says a thin white boy, one of only three guys in the class.

"Well, let's not forget you have to include observations from your journal *and* some attendant analysis. But—a play—hmmmm, maybe," Larry shrugs, keeping it going as a girl near the far wall discusses various writing styles that might be "untraditional, yet, you know, appropriate."

As he watches, he gets the "this-is-what-I-came-to-Brown-for" rush. He knows he's an oddball around campus: a fifty-one-year-old assistant professor, nontenure track, whose appreciation of teaching on this hallowed academic ground is heightened by long years of deprivation, twenty-five, in fact, slogging through eleventh-grade biology classrooms and assistant principal jobs at public high schools.

Sure, there were years he loved it, especially the eleven years in Chapel Hill, where professors' children from the University of North Carolina mixed with a manageable minority, 20 percent or so, of black and Latino kids from the town's poorer sections.

Then it fell apart, all at once. His marriage of twenty-five years collapsed. That was the main thing. Unattached, with his kids already off to college, he followed the Chapel Hill principal to Cincinnati and spent a year as an assistant principal at a well-known magnet school in the city.

That's where he read an ad in *Education Week* magazine about three-year teaching stints at Brown, with possibility of renewal. High school teachers were encouraged to apply. Larry immediately realized that competition for the fellowships would be fierce, but, beyond being a damn good teacher, he had some reasons to be hopeful. He'd had Ted Sizer, Brown's famous education professor, back when he was getting his master's in education at Harvard in the late '60s; his mix of teaching and administrating might intrigue them; and he "presented" well, with his easy, affable manner, accessible good looks (much like the fatherly, gray-haired actor William Windom), and the slightly rumpled demeanor of a professor, all tweed and oxford cotton and rep ties. He looked like he belonged at a university. People always used to say that.

He's up for renewal for a second three-year stint in a few months. He looks at his watch—5:25—about five minutes left in today's class. Better rein it in. "I think the key element some of you are not considering is the issue of skills: that you're not only here to freely express yourself on a particular subject but also to build certain time-honored skills, like clear expository writing and analysis. That's a big part of what you need to be evaluated on."

The class quiets, considering this.

"I mean that doesn't work all that well for me," says Cedric. Larry looks over. Cedric and a Latino girl from modest, inner-city origins are the two students that most intrigue him in the class, kids who are now observing life at the kind of awful schools from which they sprung. "What do you mean it doesn't work for you, Cedric?" he says softly, trying to draw out Jennings, who doesn't talk much in class.

"I don't know," Cedric says after a moment. "It's just that the things I see at my junior high school get me so angry, so passionate, that it's hard to be all intellectual, or whatever, about it."

"Why don't you write a poem about it!?" chirps Leslie from across the room, as everyone, Cedric included, begins to laugh.

"Well," Larry says, checking his watch again, so they'll all know time is up. "I'll leave it this way: if anyone wants to propose a different rubric for this midterm paper, they need to clear it with me first. Otherwise, five pages, double-spaced. See you all next time."

On a Friday afternoon a few weeks later, Larry closes the door to his small office in the education building, sits back down at his desk chair, and gazes at the phone-book-sized stack of midterm papers. Best to just shut himself in and push through the grading, however long it takes. He promised he'd hand back all the papers on Monday. By dusk, after a few hours hunched over his desk, he's well over halfway done. Most of them are what he expected—kids lifting observations from their journals, mostly mentioning exchanges between the teachers and their students, then weaving in some footnoted passages about diversity or tracking from the three books they've had to read thus far in the semester. In a few papers, he sees an occasional bit of original analysis. He marks a B at the bottom of the paper before him, scribbles a few comments, and puts it in the completed stack.

He looks down at the next one. "Oh God," he laughs, a full page of verse. Actually, he realizes, flipping it over, two full pages. He turns back to the first page and looks to the top right—"Cedric L. Jennings."

Shaking his head, he lifts his red Flair pen and begins to read.

As I gaze into this rainbow of kids
I often wonder what nature will bid.
Girls embellished in jewelry and fads,
It's hard to distinguish them from the older lads,
Boys wear earrings, pants below the waist,
In society's eyes they're indeed a disgrace.
Although these kids are in their teen years,
many have had to shed grown-up tears.
Rape victims and welfare recipients are in this array,
sometimes they're the brightest in this display.
Yet, I can no longer glory in this beautiful rainbow,
the teachers are telling them that it's time to go.
They line up in their single files,
many saying good-bye to their pals,
And, as I look a while longer, I become confused.
What was supposed to be a rainbow has become misconstrued,
There was one line of kids, who each had hooks.
The others were only concerned with their looks.
When the talking finally stops, they began a long procession.
Will the teacher or the kid be giving the lesson?

Walking through the halls can lead to dismay.
"Just say no" is the slogan of the day.
There's a poster for each case, one on every wall;
Over there's the room where they dump them all.
Inside, problems from past and present cause distress.
Is it something the teachers are really able to address?
Teachers don't have time to analyze each dilemma,
so they group the kids with proscribed curricula.
These curricula are not based on intellectual ability,
instead they target students who lack behavioral stability.
It's not that easy for these kids to behave;
Many of them, teachers think, are headed for an early grave.
But does a kid's knowledge depend on his behavior,
or should he depend on the teacher as his savior.
To meet the needs of each kid is hard,
that doesn't mean they should be called "retard."

Larry looks up and rubs his eyes; page two still to go. Jesus, he mulls, it's an epic poem. God knows he didn't expect this, but maybe he should have seen it coming. There were kids like Cedric, he recalls, at the magnet school in Cincinnati, a school that was about 60 percent white, 40 percent black. Plenty of the black kids arrived there from toxic inner-city junior high schools and were creatively gifted but short of basic skills. He used to see poems a little like this—verses, raps, or whatever—from the kids who could no more step back from the fiery elements of their poverty and blackness than some Vietnam combat vets could from the war. Everything was passed through the stark prism of their experiences and they just bled onto the page—sometimes awkwardly and, God knows, far from iambic pentameter—but often with a stunning inventiveness. Not that anyone expected their insightful effusions to take them very far; not, the joke was, until they included sections for poetry writing and personal testimony on the SATs. How, he wonders, did this Jennings kid manage to get to Brown? He flips to the second page:

> For teachers, hostility is not on the prescribed diet,
> but hope will keep the kids from causing a riot.
> Calling kids stupid is not the right way to go;
> this will stop the continuous educational flow.
> These kids are brighter than the teachers think.
> Some can audit someone's taxes in just a blink,
> Instead their minds are deteriorating with their kind,
> leaving educators in an ever tightening bind.
> These kids are crying out for attention.
> The answer is not always found in detention.
> So, will grouping them in sections solve the mystery?
> The answer may be obtained by looking at each kid's history.
> Their minds are eager, can't you see,
> these kids are yearning for real diversity.
> But teachers are always telling kids, "no you can't,"
> So the kids end up fighting and darken their chants.
> They want to be challenged, but their brains slip into ease,
> withholding their knowledge is like being a big tease.
> All this yields is a lack of respect.
> Homogeneous grouping may be the prime suspect.
>
> I must admit I'm not pleased with this picture,
> Nor the time it's taking for this painting to configure.

But a true artist must possess patience.
Developing new ideas for his latest creations
Yes, red, yellow, and orange will do,
But there's something still missing to create the perfect view.
Always looking at same hues is really no fun,
Maybe I'll just let the colors run.
This is, indeed, a great idea:
This mixture will be named the picture of the year.
With others I won't conform, to prove my expertise
My God, have I created a masterpiece?

On Monday afternoon, Larry waits until the last moment to pass out the midterm papers, not wanting the kids to be looking at them during class. He hands back Cedric's without any marks or a grade. As the class sifts out, the student comes forward.

"Why don't you come by and see me in my office and we'll talk about your paper," Larry says, making sure his tone is upbeat. "My office hours are three to five on Thursday afternoon."

Cedric stands there, stricken, holding the paper out in front of him like a burnt offering Larry might still, somehow, accept. "Don't worry, Cedric, it's nothing bad," Larry says finally, and then watches ruefully as the student slips out.

Over the next three days, Larry finds that the "poem predicament," as he dubbed it to a colleague, is regularly floating to the surface of his thoughts, making him reflective about his role as an educator, his twisting career, even his late '60s stint in the Peace Corps in Colombia, South America. He remembers how wise some of those so-called primitive villagers were, people that he, a pink-skinned young man from Harvard, was sent to help.

Sitting in his office on Thursday afternoon, he knows he needs to arrive at some decision and unearths the basic boilerplate of his role as a college professor. The rules are clear: it was a passionate, evocative poem, maybe even brilliant, but not the assignment. Yes, someone in class made a light-hearted comment about writing a poem, but he clearly stated that anyone wanting to alter the assignment needed to get it cleared first. This effort utterly disregarded the assignment. That means a **C** or maybe even an **F**. He chews on this prospect for a moment and looks to shore it up, meditating that the upholding of accepted academic standards is precisely what enables institutions like Brown to offer a diploma that has meaning, a seal showing that the recipients can master valuable skills of reasoned discourse, of deduction, exposition, and logical thinking, abilities that will help them to approach any subject, no matter how foreign, throughout their lives.

He sits for a few moments, trying to get comfortable in this posture. There's a knock on his open door. "Cedric, come in," he says, rising, and the student sits on the edge of the office's only other chair. "You know, I've thought a lot about your paper in the past couple of days," Larry opens, warming up.

"You didn't like the poem, did you?" Cedric suddenly elbows in, swallowing the last word. Larry's planned monologue is disrupted, and he discards it. "Actually, Cedric," he says softly, "I loved it. I was moved by it."

A pursed smile, almost like relief, crosses Cedric's face, and he and Larry just look at each other for a moment. The room seems warm and very quiet, and Larry, after such a long, bumpy journey to this place, suddenly feels younger and more trusting than experience should allow.

"I'm going to give you a B," he says haltingly. "But you have to understand two things. Your final research paper, which has to be according to the assignment, may carry more weight than normal in your overall grade."

Cedric nods, saying nothing, waiting for the second thing. Larry looks out the window, wanting to get it just right. "If you're going to make it here, Cedric, you'll have to find some distance from yourself and all you've been through," he says after a moment, as he leans forward, making sure their eyes meet. "The key, I think, is to put your outrage in a place where you can get at it when you need to, but not have it bubble up so much, especially when you're asked to embrace new ideas or explain what you observe to people who share none of your experiences." He stops, sensing this may be futile. "Maybe I'm not making myself clear."

"No, no, you are," Cedric says, with an eagerness that startles the teacher. "I'm understanding more about that all the time. I really am."

And Larry Wakeford, watching him go, is surprised to feel his reasonable doubts about this student's future begin to lift.

Questions for Writing and Discussion

1. What do you think of Wakeford's idea that his students and he come up with "some sort of criteria" that they can "all agree on"? Does this seem like one reasonable way to determine how a college writing assignment should

be evaluated? Consider the pros and cons and develop your own position on this practice.

2. Have you ever tried to do a formal piece of writing about something that you felt passionately about, especially something that had a personal impact on you? If not, try it. What impact does your emotional relationship with the topic have on the effectiveness of your argument? What are the benefits of writing about something you care about? What are the potential problems?

3. Explain the "poem predicament," as Wakeford called it. Would you have solved it the same way Wakeford did? If so, why? If not, why not?

4. What do you think of the advice Wakeford gives Cedric at the end of the selection? Have you ever had to find a new way to deal with an unpleasant emotion such as outrage, anger, or sadness in order to be more successful in a particular situation? Discuss the situation and what you learned from the experience.

5. Sometimes an essay isn't the most effective way to express an idea you want to get across. Consider an essay you've written in the past and discuss a situation in which your ideas might have been better expressed though poetry, visual art, film, performance or another art form. What do you think that other form would provide you that the essay doesn't? What, if anything, would be missing in the new form?

Making Connections

1. Joesph Suina in "And Then I Went to School" and Amy Tan in "Mother Tongue" both discuss the difficulties people face when they do not share a common language. Discuss a situation in which you did not share the common language of a particular group. Explain how that felt, what you did to cope with it, and what you learned from the situation. How do your situation and how you responded to it compare with Suina's and/or Tan's?

2. Thomas Oliphant's essay is the first in this chapter to mention a "values conflict," but at least one person discussed in each of the selections faces a similar conflict, some internal and some involving other people. List the values conflict present in each selection. Which of the values conflicts in this chapter do you find most compelling? Describe the conflict and explain the advice you would give to the person in order to help him or her cope with this conflict.

3. Using evidence from one or more of the selections in this chapter, attack or defend the following quotation by Thomas Wolfe: "You can't go home again." Consider the implications of this famous quotation and how it might apply to the choice a person makes to attend college.

Exploring the Web

University of Rhode Island Values Statement

http://www.uri.edu/univcol/URI101/Module_VI/uri_cornerstones.htm
This link presents the University of Rhode Island's Values Statement.
This is an example of a document that articulates some of the
cultural values of a particular college.

The Indian Pueblo Cultural Center

http://www.indianpueblo.org/intro/index.cfm
This is the official site of the Indian Pueblo Cultural Center, located
in Albuquerque, New Mexico. It provides historical information
on Pueblo people and their artistry. Information on each of the
19 Pueblo tribes as well as "authentic history and artifacts of
traditional Pueblo cultures and their contemporary art" are
featured on this site.

Institute for American Indian Education (New Mexico Institute of Bilingual Education)

http://www.nmabe.net/file/iaie.html
This site, affiliated with the National Association for Bilingual
Education, discusses the formation of the Institute for American
Indian Education, directed by Dr. Joseph Suina. According to the
site, the mission of this institute is "to provide a national forum
for educators, scholars and tribal leaders to examine the critical
education issues facing American Indian communities, explore
new ideas and appropriate instructional approaches to meet the
learning needs of American Indian students, facilitate the academic growth of American Indian students in New Mexico's
schools, and provide educational service in American Indian
communities."

James Crawford's Language Policy Website and Emporium

http://ourworld.compuserve.com/homepages/JWCRAWFORD/home.htm
This is a personal site for James Crawford, executive director of the
National Association for Bilingual Education. It includes an
extensive collection of his writings on bilingual education and
U.S. language policy as well as a wealth of definitions, discussions, and Web links relevant to the controversy surrounding
bilingual education in America.

English First

http://www.englishfirst.org
This site is owned by English First, "a national, non-profit grassroots lobbying organization" dedicated to "making English America's official language."

Cultural Bias and Standardized Testing

http://www.wilderdom.com/personality/intelligenceCulturalBias.html
This page, a part of Jim Neill's Personality and Individual Differences course at the University of Canberra, Australia, provides links, references, and information about studies done on cultural bias in standardized testing.

The Point Foundation

http://www.thepointfoundation.com
This is the official site for the Point Foundation, which "provides financial support, mentoring and hope to meritorious students who are marginalized due to sexual orientation or gender identity."

The SmartStudent Guide to Financial Aid

http://www.finaid.org/
This award-winning site, established in 1994, offers an exhaustive list of financial aid opportunities and tips for students seeking scholarships, loans, and grants. It is free for all users.

"Straddling the Blue Collar and White Collar Worlds"

http://news.minnesota.publicradio.org/features/2004/02/02_stawickie_ straddlers/
This page, a part of Minnesota Public Radio's site, includes an article about and an audio interview with Alfred Lubrano.

"First Generation College Students"

http://home.okstate.edu/homepages.nsf/toc/first_generation
This site, a part of Oklahoma State University's website, features a discussion by graduate student Billy Evans about characteristics of first-generation colleges students and support services they should consider accessing at their own colleges.

"First Generation College Students"

http://www.ericdigests.org/1992-1/first.htm
This site features an article by Karin Petersen Hsiao that touches on the
idea that Alfred Lubrano focuses on—the idea that first-generation
college students are straddling "two cultures." This article places
special emphasis on initiatives by community colleges to serve this
population.

"First Generation Students Bridge the Gap"

http://www.cnn.com/2004/EDUCATION/01/21/first.to.college.ap/
This article, published by CNN.com, follows two first-generation college students as they struggle and strive to be successful during
their first semester as college students.

A Hope in the Unseen

http://www.ronsuskind.com/newsite/hopeunseen/
This site provides information about Ron Suskind and *A Hope in the
Unseen* as well as Suskind's other works. This site includes an
update about what happened to Cedric after his first year at Brown
University.

CHAPTER 2

A Day in the Life: Opportunities and Challenges In and Out of the Classroom

Overview

At this point, you probably realize that being a member of college culture means that some basic things about your life are changing, such as how, where, and with whom you choose to spend your time. You may also be noticing new opportunities available to you. New friendships may be developing; you may be confronted with new ideas, and not just in your classes. Perhaps you're meeting people who have grown up in such unusual places and with such different experiences from yours that you are excited, angered, or intimidated by the way they see the world.

By now, your choices, even small ones, are impacting your college's culture. You are a new member of this world, rather than a tourist visiting a strange land called college. You might have joined a club, attended some lectures, and enjoyed a sporting event or a party. On some days, you feel like you've been here for years. On others, you might as well have been dropped onto another planet for all the unexpected possibilities that you see.

As you read this chapter, consider the insights, opportunities, and challenges you are facing as a result of being a part of your college's culture. What will you do with these insights and how will you confront these challenges and opportunities?

MAKING IT MATTER

Consider the value of friendship in your life. Has the nature of your friendships changed as you have grown older? Do your friendships with men differ from those with women? If so, to what do you attribute this difference?

BREAKING IT DOWN

Tesich gives a number of examples to illustrate his thesis and develop his comparison. Consider what unique point each example is making. Would this essay be as effective without any one of these examples? Would it be more effective with an additional example?

Focusing on Friends
STEVE TESICH

Steve Tesich (1943–1996). He was a playwright and screenwriter, best known for winning an Academy Award for the film Breaking Away *in 1979. He wrote the following essay in 1983.*

————————◆————————

When I think of people who were my good friends, I see them all, as I do everything else from my life, in cinematic terms. The camera work is entirely different for men and women.

I remember all the women in almost extreme close-ups. The settings are different—apartments, restaurants—but they're all interiors, as if I had never spent a single minute with a single woman outside. They're looking right at me, these women in these extreme close-ups; the lighting is exquisite, worthy of a Fellini or Fosse film, and their lips are moving. They're telling me something important or reacting to something even more important that I've told them. It's the kind of movie where you tell people to keep quiet when they chew their popcorn too loudly.

The boys and men who were my friends are in an entirely different movie. No close-ups here. No exquisite lighting. The camera work is rather shaky but the background is moving. We're going somewhere, on foot, on bicycles, in cars. The ritual of motion, or action, makes up for the inconsequential nature of the dialogue. It's a much sloppier film, this film that is not really a film but a memory of real friends: Slobo, Louie, Sam. Male friends. I've loved all three of them. I assumed they knew this, but I never told them.

Quite the contrary is true in my female films. In close-up after close-up, I am telling every woman who I ever loved that I love her, and then lingering on yet another close-up of her face for a reaction. There is a perfectly appropriate musical score playing while I wait. And if I wait long enough, I get an answer. I am loved. I am not loved. Language clears up the suspense. The emotion is nailed down.

Therein lies the difference, I think, between my friendships with men and with women. I can tell women I love them. Not only can I tell them, I am compulsive about it. I can hardly wait to tell them. But I can't tell the men. I just can't. And they can't tell me. Emotions are never nailed down. They run wild, and I and my male friends chase after them, on foot, on bicycles, in cars, keeping the quarry in sight but never catching up.

My first friend was Slobo. I was still living in Yugoslavia at the time, and not far from my house there was an old German truck left abandoned after the war. It had no wheels. No windshield. No doors. But the steering wheel was intact. Slobo and I flew to America in that truck. It was our airplane. Even now, I remember the background moving as we took off down the street, across Europe, across the Atlantic. We were inseparable: the best of friends. Naturally, not one word concerning the nature of our feelings for one another was ever exchanged. It was all done in actions.

The inevitable would happen at least once a day. As we were flying over the Atlantic, there came, out of nowhere, that wonderful moment: engine failure! "We'll have to bail out," I shouted. "A-a-a-a-a!" Slobo made the sound of a failing engine. Then he would turn and look me in the eye: "I can't swim," he'd say. "Fear not." I put my hand on his shoulder. "I'll drag you to shore." And, with that, both of us would tumble out of the truck onto the dusty street. I swam through the dust. Slobo drowned in the dust, coughing, gagging. "Sharks!" he cried. But I always saved him. The next day the ritual would be repeated, only then it would be my turn to say "I can't swim," and Slobo would save me. We saved each other from certain death over a hundred times, until finally a day came when I really left for America with my mother and sister. Slobo and I stood at the train station. We were there to say goodbye, but, since we weren't that good at saying things and since he couldn't save me, he just cried until the train started to move.

The best friend I had in high school was Louie. It now seems to me that I was totally monogamous when it came to male friends. I would have several girl friends but only one real male friend. Louie was it at that time. We were both athletes, and one day we decided to "run till we drop." We just wanted to know what it was like. Skinny Louie set the pace as we ran around our high-school track. Lap after lap. Four laps to a mile. Mile after mile we ran. I had the reputation as being a big-time jock. Louie didn't. But this was Louie's day. There was a bounce in his step and, when he turned back to look at me, his eyes were gleaming with the thrill of it all. I finally dropped. Louie still looked fresh; he seemed capable, on that day, of running forever. But we were the best of friends, and so he stopped. "That's it," he lied. "I couldn't go another step farther." It was an act of love. Naturally, I said nothing.

Louie got killed in Vietnam. Several weeks after his funeral, I went to his mother's house, and, because she was a woman, I tried to tell her how much I had loved her son. It was not a good scene. Although I was telling the truth, my words sounded like lies. It was all very painful and embarrassing. I kept thinking how sorry I was that I had never told Louie himself.

Sam is my best friend now, and has been for many years. A few years ago, we were swimming at a beach in East Hampton. The Atlantic! The very Atlantic I had flown over in my German truck with Slobo. We had swum out pretty far from the shore when both of us simultaneously thought we spotted a shark. Water is not only a good conductor of electricity but of panic as well. We began splashing like madmen toward shore. Suddenly, at the height of my panic, I realized how much I loved my friend, what an irreplaceable friend he was, and, although I was the faster swimmer, I fell back to protect him. Naturally, the shark in the end proved to be imaginary. But not my feelings for my friend. For several days after that I wanted to share my discovery with him, to tell him how much I loved him. Fortunately, I didn't.

I say fortunately because on reflection, there seems to be sufficient evidence to indicate that, if anybody was cheated and short-changed by me, it was the women, the girls, the very recipients of my uncensored emotions. Yes, I could hardly wait to tell them I loved them. I did love them. But since I told them, something stopped. The emotion was nailed down, but, with it, the enthusiasm and the energy to prove it was nailed down, too. I can remember my voice saying to almost all of them, at one time or another: "I told you I love you. What else do you want?" I can now recoil in the impatient hostility of that voice but I can't deny it was mine.

The tyranny of self-censorship forced me, in my relations with male friends, to seek alternatives to language. And just because I could never be sure they understood exactly how I felt about them, I was forced to look for ways to prove it. That is,

I now think, how it should be. It is time to make adjustments. It is time to pull back the camera, free the women I know, and myself, from those merciless close-ups and have the background move.

Questions for Writing and Discussion

1. Characterize the qualities of your closest friendships and consider what they have in common and how they are different. What accounts for the similarities and differences? Is it your friends' ages, genders, attitudes, cultural backgrounds, or something else that makes the friendships vary? How much of the difference can you attribute to yourself? Why do you think you behave similarly or differently with these different friends?

2. When Tesich writes about his memories of playing in an abandoned truck with Slobo, he states "Slobo and I flew to America in that truck." Develop a scene, or a series of scenes, in which you take on the point of view you had as a child—pretending or using your imagination. What does this scene tell you about what you valued as a child? Are there any connections between these values and what you value as an adult?

3. Describe a situation in which you were particularly proud or somewhat embarrassed about how you behaved toward a friend. What, if anything, did you, and/or your friend, learn from the situation?

4. While most of the body paragraphs of this essay focus on his friendships with males, Tesich spends a lot of time talking about female friends at the beginning of this essay and then returns to this topic at the end. Why do you think he has chosen to structure his essay this way?

5. Did the conclusion that Tesich reaches in this essay surprise you? Why or why not?

MAKING IT MATTER

Have you ever used the Internet to do research about a date, potential friend, or professor? Would you be comfortable with a potential employer, date, or professor using the Internet to learn more about you?

BREAKING IT DOWN

Dince presents a number of viewpoints in this article. If you were writing this article would you have sought out any additional viewpoints? Why or why not?

Could Your Facebook Profile Throw a Wrench in Your Future?

REBECCA DINCE

Rebecca Dince graduated from Tufts University in 2006. As a student, she served as the Features Editor for the Tufts Daily, *where this article was first printed.*

———————————— ✦ ————————————

When the wildly popular Web site Facebook.com was created by Harvard University student Mark Zuckerberg in 2004, it began as a safe haven for college students to express themselves through their profiles and to connect with each other.

But with many students revealing such personal information as addresses, cell phone numbers, schedules and sexual preferences on Facebook, privacy issues have been raised. Campus administrators, university police departments, admissions offices, parents and even employers have begun to peruse Facebook in order to check up on students.

In order to sign up for Facebook, all that employers need is an e-mail address ending in ".edu"—meaning that anyone who is a recent college graduate or who has an alumni e-mail address can sign up.

This easy access to the site has resulted in employers figuring out that Facebook could prove useful when conducting background searches on graduating seniors that are applying for jobs.

One recent Tufts graduate working as a consultant in New York City, who requested anonymity, said that his employer told him "to check Facebook to find a kid who was applying for a job at the company." The employer "said he wanted to see if his profile supported what he thought of this kid."

According to Assistant Director of Career Services, Nicole Anderson, "We have heard from alumni in business, law and finance that they are aware of websites such as these."

"They have probably heard about the sites from younger employees in their organizations who are more familiar with the sites. Even though senior employees may not be the ones checking Facebook, you can be sure that they may ask their junior employees to look online," Anderson added.

"I know that when [my girlfriend] was applying for her job in computer programming, they Googled her before the interview," said Rob Fishell (LA"05) who now works for Starwood Hotels and Resorts. "They only told her about it three months after she got hired."

"It's definitely an emerging issue for career services, given that students use websites like this so frequently, and that content is questionable. This topic is popping up at conferences in higher education," Anderson added.

Aware that many students post pictures and descriptions of their drunken debauchery on the site, administrators at Tufts began offering seminars in Facebook propriety last year during freshman orientation.

"We have always warned students about what they put on the Web. We warn them about the content of their own websites, even if they have not chosen to make this website available to employers," Anderson said. "We have started to warn them about anything an employer could discover in the public domain."

But the use of the site in this manner also raises ethical concerns.

"It seems to me that people who look at sites such as Facebook in order to, in effect, spy on students are taking advantage of the internet in a way that's not all that different from the way that sexual predators exploit it," said Assistant Professor of Philosophy Nancy Bauer, who teaches Introduction to Ethics.

"Obviously, employers or administrators who look at these sites are not breaking any laws, but they are fully aware that they are covertly looking at information that students might never voluntarily give them and then, at least in some cases, using that information in a way that hurts the students," Bauer said.

"I don't think that employers could find anything in my profile to use against me but I still don't think they should do it," said senior Jessica Powers, who has been hired as a financial consultant in New York for next year. "It's not a valid source for background checks. It seems like they stoop to a low level if they actually do that."

"I also think it says something about the firm if they do it," Powers added.

"We use systems like Facebook to share uncensored aspects of our life with the college community, thinking nothing more of it," said senior Ajaita Shah, who one day hopes to go into politics.

"However, now that this system is being used as a way to spy on our lives for the professional sphere, we are all in danger." "Clearly we'd all have to become much more aware of our actions, what gets posted online, and reconsider sharing anything at all," Shah said. "But what's more obnoxious is that they are doing this without us being informed. It's a direct infringement upon our rights."

"This is not like a parent sneaking into a kid's room and reading her diary—when an employer, in particular, is involved, one could hardly argue that the motivation in trolling websites that are set up for social purposes is to promote the potential employees' interests," Bauer said. "The motivation, rather, is to take advantage of a certain naivete on the part of students. That's exploitation, and any plausible code of ethics is going to find it, at bare minimum, disturbing."

Some of Facebook's security features include a degree lock that allows users to choose who can view their profile on a social network. By choosing the third degree, the person can only view their profile if they are a "friend of a friend of a friend."

"Safety and privacy concerns are one of our top priorities—take a look at the extensive privacy settings that we've had from the outset as evidence, and as far as identity theft, we're confident that our members are intelligent enough not to give out any personal information that they want to be public," said Facebook spokesman Chris Hughes.

"If any user does use the network inappropriately, we'll throw that person off the network," he added.

But according to Hughes, while the site was created for students, there is nothing that prohibits college faculty and administrators from using the site.

"They have the legal right to use it because it is a public forum," he said.

Hughes said it seems to be legal for college administrators to look on Facebook profiles for illegal activities such as underage drinking or illegal drug use. But, he added, "that wasn't our first intention for creating the Facebook."

"I think it's 100 percent unethical. I don't have anything in my profile I wouldn't want people to see, but a lot of people do," said senior Jeremy Kirbal, who is currently applying for jobs in the financial sector. "A personal profile is meant for personal use only."

Students, however, seem to be divided on the issue of Facebook privacy. While some are irate that their college hijinx may be used against them, others seem to have accepted that confidentiality may be impossible in the age of the Internet.

"My first reaction is that snooping on the internet for background info is sort of nosy and unprofessional," said senior Dena Miller. "But really, I don't think students should put things on public Internet sites that they don't want seen by others—employers included."

"It's a personality test. What you have on sites like Facebook is just another way the company can do behavioral analysis of you," Fishell said. "If you are going to apply for a big time job with a straight edge company, they want to know every detail they can about who you are, and MySpace or Facebook can tell them a lot about you."

"And from that they can determine if they like you," Fishell added. "I mean, you're putting tons of info about yourself out on the web for anyone to see and it can definitely affect your future."

"It's worrisome that students aren't aware that in posting things about themselves on Internet sites—even sites to which there is in principle limited access—they are in effect abrogating their privacy and making themselves vulnerable," Bauer said.

"That students are naive does not mean that they are to be blamed for what employers are doing, or even that employers are morally off the hook," she continued. "But its does mean that, like it or not, students are in effect asking for trouble."

"The Internet is for public consumption," Anderson agreed. "What a student puts on their own page, or what others choose to add to it, is out there for the world to see and to subsequently evaluate.

"Students put much effort and time into preparing for their job search," she added. "It's unfortunate that they might unknowingly damage their chance for a job or internship offer. Students can be naive in their job search, not realizing that subtle signs or gestures can lead to an employer's hesitancy or rejection."

"Very often, our job as career counselors is to teach students how to investigate companies and how to learn things about them that is not common knowledge," Anderson continued. "Students don't necessarily take our advice, but it looks like the employers have."

Questions for Writing and Discussion

1. If you are a user of Facebook, you might have discovered that there have been changes in some of this site's features since Rebecca Dince's article was published. These changes affect membership to the social network and security settings. If you are not a Facebook user or are not immediately aware of the specific updates this site has made, go to http://www.facebook.com and research the changes. Using what you have learned through your research or participation on this site or other social networking sites, develop an argument for why the main point of this essay is still valid, no longer valid, or somewhat valid.

2. Do you have a personal website? Have you posted personal information about yourself on a site designed for social networking? Where do you draw the line about what you will make public in this forum? Write an essay that provides advice about revealing public information online based on your criteria for doing so.

3. Write an essay about a situation in which someone learned something about you that you did not personally tell him or her. Was the information accurate? Did you feel that your privacy was violated? What have you done since then to make this less likely to occur?

4. Dince attempts to look at several sides of this controversial issue. Who do you think is responsible? Should employers refrain from doing research on social networking sites or on the Internet in general, or should people post only information they are comfortable with employers seeing? To what extent do you see these employers as unethical? To what extent are students being naive?

5. Do you think it is ethical for students to access sites that post information written by other students about their professors? To what degree is this similar to the situation discussed in this selection? To what degree is it different?

MAKING IT MATTER

Before you came to college, did you have an image of what the "party scene" would be like? Is the amount of drinking that you see on your campus, or among students off-campus, what you expected to find at your college? To what extent, if any, do you see this as a problem?

BREAKING IT DOWN

Sink uses both specific examples and statistical evidence to make her point. As you read, consider the effects that this choice has on her argument.

Drinking Deaths Draw Attention to Old Campus Problem

MINDY SINK

Mindy Sink is a Denver-based contributor to the New York Times, *where this article was originally published.*

———————— ✦ ————————

Lynn G. Bailey, 18, a freshman at the University of Colorado here, spent his last night chugging whiskey and wine as part of an initiation ceremony with his fraternity brothers. Left by his friends to sleep it off, he died from alcohol poisoning.

Less than two weeks earlier and an hour's drive away, Samantha Spady, 19, a sophomore at Colorado State University in Fort Collins, died of alcohol poisoning after an evening out with friends in which she drank the equivalent of 30 to 40 beers and shots.

In the aftermath of these deaths this fall, university officials and community leaders are joining forces, rather than pointing fingers, and are looking at how they can take responsibility together to prevent alcohol abuse.

"It was the straw that broke the camel's back," said a Boulder city councilman and the deputy mayor, Tom Eldridge, of the back-to-back deaths and years of tension built up in neighborhoods adjacent to the campus.

The University of Colorado is still dealing with damage to its image after accusations of rape involving football players and recruits in recent years. Many of those accusations also involved drinking, legally or not, at private parties and bars. Some critics questioned what kind of message it sent to students that the athletic director, Dick Tharp, was also an owner of Liquor Mart, the town's largest liquor store. Boulder and Fort Collins have a history of alcohol-fueled riots and out-of-control parties often combined with underage drinking despite years of the universities' offering awareness programs, participating in studies to reduce campus drinking, selective banning of alcohol on campus and more punitive measures, like suspension and calling parents.

"The community and the campus both have to admit they have a problem," said Dr. Richard Yoast, director of an American Medical Association program to reduce high-risk drinking. "I think it's very important that they work together."

To that end, business owners, neighborhood associations, student groups and college and community leaders are meeting.

One month after Mr. Bailey's death, the Boulder City Council unanimously passed a resolution to review alcohol licensing policies, zoning laws and code enforcement as ways to decrease binge drinking by college students. In Fort Collins, beer sales have been banned at football games, alcohol consumption is banned in fraternities and sororities, and a task force that includes the state's lieutenant governor and the local police chief is studying ways to reduce alcohol abuse.

"Certainly when we have an event like this, and when we heard of the death in Fort Collins first, it's a lightning rod and focuses our attention," said the Boulder mayor, Mark Ruzzin. "Between the university and the city we have evolved our thinking that students are community members, so we've pretty much dissolved that jurisdictional line between university and the city."

Both Ms. Spady and Mr. Bailey died in fraternity houses after drinking at private parties or in the mountains all evening. (The local chapters of those fraternities have been closed indefinitely.) Ms. Spady had a blood alcohol level of .436 percent, over five times the .08 percent that is the national standard for drunken driving, and Mr. Bailey's was .328. The minimum drinking age is 21; both were teenagers.

Experts say that these deaths represent just a fraction of the problem of binge drinking on college campuses: there have been three more alcohol poisoning deaths this year, involving college students in Arkansas, Virginia and Oklahoma, and a death at Colorado College in Colorado Springs in which a student fell from a window after hours of drinking. According to a 2002 study by the National Institute on Alcohol Abuse and Alcoholism, approximately 1,400 college students 18 to 24 die annually as a result of alcohol abuse. While most of those deaths are from traffic accidents, about 300 are from unintentional injuries that include alcohol poisoning.

"It's only through luck that we haven't had this become a weekly occurrence," said Bob Maust, chairman of the Standing Committee on Substance Abuse at the University of Colorado. I've been doing this for 35 years, and I see the results every week of near misses."

Mr. Maust said that what was less studied or publicized were the many college students who did survive near-lethal intoxication after being rushed to emergency rooms by friends.

A Boulder city councilman, Will Toor, said that while he supported making changes to help prevent alcohol abuse, he urged caution. "I am somewhat concerned that past attempts—from the federal level to the local level—have made things worse," Mr. Toor said, adding that campus restrictions on drinking had pushed students away from adult-controlled environments and even into drinking harder alcohol.

One of the issues being looked at here is the high density of liquor stores and bars around college campuses and the frequent discounts the businesses offer.

"The cheaper the drinks, the more problems," Dr. Yoast said, referring to offers of two for one or free drinks for women at bars near campuses.

But some local business owners say they are being blamed unfairly.

"I don't think the liquor stores are the problem," said Russell Harverson, general manager of Rose Hill Wine and Spirits, a store one block from campus here. "These kids are away from home for the first time and not taught to drink responsibly. We do our darnedest not to sell to minors."

Mr. Harverson spoke as he was putting up signs for his shot glasses and beer mugs with the college logo on them.

Brian Lane, 22, who stopped at the store on a Friday morning to buy an 18-pack of beer for himself and friends that night, said that his own drinking had decreased from when he was a freshman and that more restrictions would not solve the problem.

"I think it's more individual responsibility," Mr. Lane said. "There is plenty of stuff to do in Boulder besides drinking."

Questions for Writing and Discussion

1. Why do you think Sink chooses to open her article the way she does? What effect does that opening have on you as a reader?

2. Most people would agree that excessive drinking that leads to death and injury is a problem that needs to be dealt with, but the causes of this problem are debatable. Make a list of some of the causes that Sink suggests in her article. Based on your experience at your college, which of these causes seem most reasonable? Which seem least reasonable?

Support your response with evidence from what you have witnessed or experienced.

3. Do you think the partnership of local "business owners, neighborhood associations, student groups and college and community leaders," as suggested in the reading, would have a positive impact on this problem? Why or why not?

4. To what degree do you think students themselves are responsible for the amount of drinking that goes on at and around their colleges? What steps do you take to prevent the kind of problems that occurred at the University of Colorado?

5. Select one of the causes that Sink mentions in her article and research the influence it has on the drinking habits of students at your college. You may want to apply your research to another school as well and compare the two. Consider some conclusions you may draw from this comparison to suggest a solution to the problem at one or both of the schools, if you feel a solution is needed.

MAKING IT MATTER

What do you think is an appropriate way to learn about sexuality and the ramifications (positive and negative) of being sexually active? Was learning to be fearful about sex an element of your education? If so, do you think that was a useful strategy?

BREAKING IT DOWN

How would you describe Daum's tone in the piece? To answer that question, ask yourself how she feels about her own sex and AIDS education.

We're Lying: Safe Sex and White Lies in the Time of AIDS

MEGHAN DAUM

Meghan Daum is the author of the novel The Quality of Life Report *and the essay collection* My Misspent Youth *and writes a weekly column for the* Los Angeles Times. *This article first appeared in* New York Times Magazine.

◆

We grew up with simple, cozy absolutes. Our high school educators knew what they were doing. They taught what they were taught to teach. . . . They told us how to act like the "adults we were becoming," never to drink and drive, never to "experiment" with "cannabis," and never to have sex or even go to third base as the result would be emotional trauma of unimaginable proportions, not to mention pregnancy which could mean nothing other than ruined lives, missed proms, the prophecy of the sack of flour we carried around for health class finally realized.

It wasn't until college that I heard the AIDS speeches. Suddenly we were on our own and didn't have to bring the car back by midnight, so it seemed incumbent upon all those dorm mothers and counselors to give us the straight talk, to tell us never, ever to have sex without condoms unless we wanted to die, that's right *die*, shrivel overnight, vomit up our futures, pose a threat to others (and they'd seen it happen, oh yes they had).

Suddenly, pregnancy's out the window concern-wise. It's a lesser evil, a math class rather than a physics class, Chaucer and not Middle English survey. Even those other diseases, the ones they had mentioned in health class, like gonorrhea and even the incurable herpes, seem inconsequential. AIDS is foremost in our malleable minds, a phantom in our not-yet-haunted houses. They tell us we can get it, and we believe them and vow to protect ourselves, and intend (really, truly) to stick by that, until we don't because we just can't, because it's just not fair, because our sense of entitlement exceeds our sense of vulnerability. So, we blow off precaution again and again and then we get scared and get an HIV test and everything turns out okay and we run out of the clinic, pamphlets in hand, eyes cast upwards, saying we'll never be stupid again. But of course we are stupid, again and again. And the subsequent testing is always for the same reasons and with the same results and soon it becomes more like fibbing about SAT scores ten years after the fact than lying about practicing unsafe sex, a lie which sounds like such a breach in contract with oneself that we might as well be talking about putting a loaded gun to our heads every night and attempting to use our trigger finger to clean the wax from our ear.

I have been tested for HIV three times; the opportunities for testing were there, so I took them, forgetting, each time, the fear and nausea that always ensues before the results come back, those minutes spent in a publicly funded waiting room staring at a video loop about "living with" this thing that kills you. I've been negative each time, which is not surprising in retrospect, since I am not a member of a "high risk group." Yet I continue to go into relationships with the safest of intentions and often discard precaution at some random and tacitly agreed-upon juncture. Perhaps this is a shocking admission, but my hunch is that I'm not the only one doing this. My suspicion is, in fact, that very few of us—"us" being the demographic frequently charged with thinking we're immortal, the population accused of being cynical and lazy and weak for lack of a war draft and altogether unworthy of the label "adult"—have really responded to the AIDS crisis in the way the federal government and the educational system would like to think. My guess is that we're all but ignoring it and that almost anyone who claims otherwise is lying.

It's not that we're reckless. It's more that we're grasping at straws, trying like hell to feel good in a time when half of us seem to be on Prozac and the rest of us have probably been told that we need it. When it comes down to it, it's hard to use condoms. Even as a woman, I know this. Maybe the risk is a substitute for thrills we're missing in other areas of life. Maybe there's something secretly energizing about flirting with death for a night and then checking six months later to see if we've survived. This, at least, constitutes intensity of experience, a real, tangible interaction with raw fear. It's so much more than what we get most of the time, subject as we are to the largely protected, government approved, safety first-ness of American society. For my peers and myself, it's generally safe to assume that our homes will not be bombed while we sleep, that our flight will not crash, that we will make the daily round trip from our beds to the office and back again without deadly intervention somewhere in between. We live in the land of side impact air bags, childproof caps on vitamins, "do not ingest" warnings on deodorant bottles. We don't intend to die in childbirth. Even for those of us, like myself, who live in cities, who read *USA Today* polls that we'll probably get mugged eventually, who vaguely mull over the fact that the person shot on the corner last week could have been us, fear continues to exist in the abstract. We've had it pretty cushy. We've been shielded from most forms of undoing by parents and educational institutions and health insurance. But AIDS is housed in its own strange caveat of intimate conversations among friends and those occasional sleepless nights when it occurs to us to wonder about it, upon which that dark paranoia sets in and those catalogs of who we've done it with and who they might have done it with and oh-my-god-I'll-surely-die seem to project themselves onto the ceiling the way fanged monsters did when we were kids. But we fall asleep and then we wake up. And nothing's changed except our willingness to forget about it, which is, in fact, almost everything.

Much of the discourse surrounding AIDS in the early 1990s was informed by a male homosexual community, which, in the interests of prevention, assumed an alarmist position. In a *Village Voice* review of two books about the AIDS crisis and gay men, writer Michael Warner described HIV negative status as "living around, under, and next to crisis for that indefinite, rest-of-your-life blank stretch of time." And even though he is speaking largely of the crisis as it relates to gay men, he points out that for homosexuals and heterosexuals alike, "negative status is always in jeopardy and has to be preserved through effort." These sorts of statements are, in many ways, a legitimate tactic for HIV prevention in the gay community, which has been devastated by the disease in staggering proportions. But when words like "crisis" and "effort" are aimed at the heterosexual population as well, a lot of us tend to stop listening. What constitutes strenuous effort for one person may be routine behavior for another. For better or worse, guidelines for HIV prevention among straight people are often a matter of interpretation.

The message is that trusting anyone is itself an irresponsible act, that having faith, in an intimate partner, particularly women in relation to men, is a symptom of such profound naiveté that we're obviously not mature enough to be having sex anyway. That this reasoning runs counter to almost any feminist ideology—the ideology that told us, at least back in the 70s, that women should feel free to ask men on dates and wear jeans and have orgasms—is an admission that few AIDS-concerned citizens are willing to make. Two decades after *The Joy of Sex* made sexual pleasure accessible to both genders and the pill put a government approved stamp on premarital sex, we're still being told not to trust each other. Women are being told that if they believe a man who claims he's healthy, they're just plain stupid. Men are wary of any woman who seems one or more steps away from virgin-hood. Twenty years after the sexual revolution, we seem to be in a sleepier, sadder time than the 1950s. We've entered a period where mistrust equals responsibility, where paranoia signifies health.

Since I spent all of the 1970s under the age of ten, I've never known a significantly different sexual and social climate. Supposedly this makes it easier. Health educators and AIDS activists like to think that people of my generation can be made to unlearn what we never knew, to break the reckless habits we didn't actually form. But what we have learned thoroughly is how not to enjoy ourselves. Just like our mothers, whose adolescences were haunted by the abstract taboo of "nice" girls versus some other kind of girl, my contemporaries and I are again discouraged from doing what feels good. As it was with our mothers, the onus falls largely on the women. We know that it's much easier for women to contract HIV from a man than the other way around. We know that an "unsafe" man generally means someone who's shot drugs or slept with other men, or possibly slept with prostitutes. We find ourselves wondering about these things over dinner dates. We look for any hints of homosexual tendencies, any references to a hypodermic moment. We try to catch him in the lie we've been told he'll tell.

What could be sadder? When I was a young teenager,. . . I looked forward to growing up and being able to do what I wanted, to live without a curfew, to talk on the phone as long as I wanted, and even to find people whom I could love and trust. But trust is out of vogue. We're not allowed to believe anyone anymore. And the reason we're not isn't because of AIDS but because of the lack of specificity in the anxiety that ripples around the disease. The information about AIDS that was formerly known as "awareness" has been subsumed into the unfortunate—and far less effective—incarnation of "style." As in *Kids,* where violence and ignorance are shown so relentlessly that we don't notice it by the end, AIDS awareness has become so much a part of the pop culture that not only is it barely noticeable, it is ineffectual. MTV runs programs about safe sex that are virtually identical to episodes of "The Real World." Madonna pays self-righteous lip service to safe sex despite basketball star Dennis Rodman's claim that she refused to let him wear a condom during their tryst. A print advertisement for the Benetton clothing company features a collage of hundreds of tiny photographs of young people, some of whom are shaded and have the word AIDS written across their faces. Many are white and blond and have the tousled, moneyed look common to more traditional fashion spreads or even yearbooks from colleges like the one I attended. There is no text other than the company's slogan. There is no explanation of how these faces were chosen, no public statement of whether these people actually have the disease or not. I called Benetton for clarification and was told that the photographs were supposed to represent people from all over the world and that no one shown was known to be HIV positive: Just as I suspected, the advertisement was essentially a work of art, which meant I could interpret the image any way I liked. This is how the deliverers of the safer sex message shoot themselves in the foot. By choosing a hard sell over actual information, people like me are going to believe what we want to believe, which, of course, is the thing that isn't so scary. So, I turn the page.

Heterosexuals are being sent vague signals. We're being told that if we are sufficiently vigilant, we'll probably be all right. We're told to assume the worst and not to invite disaster by hoping for the best. We're encouraged to keep our fantasies on tight reins, otherwise we'll lose control of the whole buggy, and no one will be able to say we weren't warned.

But I've been warned over and over again and there's still no visible cautionary tale. Since I'm as provincial and self-absorbed as the next person, I probably won't truly begin to take the AIDS crisis personally until I see either someone like me succumb to it or concrete statistics that show that we are. Until then, my peers and I are left with generalized anxiety, a low-grade fear and anger that resides at the core of everything we do. Our attitudes have been affected by the disease in that we're scared, but our behavior has stayed largely the same. The result of this is a corrosion of the soul, a chronic dishonesty and fear of ourselves that will, for us, likely do more damage than the disease itself. In this world, peace of mind is a Utopian concept.

Questions for Writing and Discussion

1. Do you agree with Daum's point that the result of her generation's AIDS education is "a corrosion of the soul, a chronic dishonesty, and a fear of [themselves] that will . . . do more damage than the disease itself"? Why or why not?

2. Most would agree that Daum's point of view is an honest but controversial one. What are some aspects of her experience that have led her to develop this perspective?

3. Daum suggests that the emotional and psychological consequences associated with what she and her peers have been taught about AIDS prevention is too high a price. Identify the emotional and psychological issues she discusses. Do you agree with her? Why or why not?

4. Who is the "we" Daum often refers to in her article? Do you see yourself as part of this "we"? Why or why not?

5. Do you feel that sex education should be taught in public schools? If so, at what age should this begin and what should be taught? Do some research on this issue (see relevant sites in this chapter's "Exploring the Web" as a starting point) and come to an informed decision about what type of sex education, if any, you would support in your community's schools.

MAKING IT MATTER

Do you notice a difference between the way men and women view the role of a college education? If so, how do you account for the difference? If not, how do you account for the trend that fewer men than women are attending college today?

BREAKING IT DOWN

Consider Rodriguez's choice to use so many quotations from people she interviewed. Why are quotes from these particular people valuable to the reader's understanding?

Universities Seeing a Gender Gap in Enrollments

ERIN MALLANTS RODRIGUEZ

Erin Mallants Rodriguez wrote this article for the Miami Herald, *to which she is a regular contributor.*

———————— ✦ ————————

It's a trend that continues to grow—more women are attending college after high school, but fewer men are enrolling.

At Barry University, only 28 percent of undergraduate students are men. At Florida Memorial University, 42 percent of the student population in fall 2004 was male. At Miami Dade College, 38 percent of students in fall 2003 were men. At both the University of Miami and St. Thomas University, men made up 43 percent of the freshman class for 2004.

At Broward Community College, only 35 percent of the students were men last fall. At Nova University, men accounted for only 30 percent of undergraduates.

"It's a reflection of people graduating from high school," said Lydia Amy, St. Thomas University's dean of enrollment management. "This is like a domino effect—and it progresses."

Andre Lightbourn, director of admissions at St. Thomas University, agrees that the problem begins at the high school level. He says college does not appeal to many of the male high school students he encounters.

"Even when you sit down with the students—the females are more astute and savvy with the process," Lightbourn said. "Inevitably, what I think will happen is that more women will occupy the CEO positions and become more of a commodity down the road."

Helen Corpuz, Barry's director of undergraduate admission, sees several possible reasons for the gender gap.

"The increasing job opportunities in fields related to information technology play a factor among college-age males selecting a more vocational or technical, nontraditional education," she said.

According to the National Center for Education Statistics, men earned 42 percent of all degrees in the academic year 2002–2003. What's more, researchers believe women are more likely than men to enter college later in life.

So where are the men?

Albert Cruz, 24, of Hialeah, tried going to college after graduating from high school, but says it was too much.

"I was trying to work and go to school—and work would interfere with my classes," said Cruz, who worked his way up to store manager at an automotive shop. "I needed to make more money and at the same time my job was becoming more demanding."

Cruz had planned to earn a degree in business administration, but found out sometimes it's not what you know, but who you know. For five months, he's been working as a sales consultant at Esserman Nissan in Miami Lakes.

"One of my customers got me this job," he said. "I've always liked working with people, so this is great. I'm making more money than some people who go to college. The income is unlimited."

When asked if he ever plans to go back to school, Cruz says probably not. He's happy with his career.

"It's not for everybody," Cruz said. "I'm a hustler. This is not the type of career where you can sit down and expect deals to come to you. You have to go out there and get them."

At Miami Dade College, where the total student population is the highest in South Florida (almost 60,000 attend), the Restart Center at the Kendall campus serves both men and women who want to go back to college, offering specialized counseling, mentoring and child-care vouchers.

Dr. Nora Hendrix, president of the InterAmerican Campus at Miami Dade College, says the push to get both men and women in the classroom will always be there.

"College education is no longer something you do just after high school," Hendrix said. "You always have to have services for them. We see people coming to school their entire lives."

Corpuz also notes more women are applying to college than ever before—and, in general, women have an advantage once inside the classroom.

"Females tend to be better performing students, perhaps due to the level of maturity," Corpuz said. "Since many colleges and universities are seeking to increase academic quality, female applicants are more readily being accepted because of their stronger academic profiles—which can also lead to better opportunities for scholarships and grants."

Questions for Writing and Discussion

1. Rodriguez cites some reasons why fewer men might be attending college. Can you think of any more? Support your response with examples from your experience or the experiences of those you know.

2. Often, when a group is identified as being underrepresented, colleges will develop programs or incentives to attract that group of people to apply. Traditionally, these programs have targeted groups who have been seen as underprivileged or discriminated against. Do you think special programs or incentives would be an appropriate way to attract more men to college campuses? If so, what types of programs or incentives would be appropriate, and should they be available to all students or just men?

3. Albert Cruz says that he chose to forgo college for two reasons: "work would interfere with . . . classes" and he's already making "more money than some people who go to college." Do you think Cruz's reasons are legitimate and

well thought-out? If he were your friend, how would you have advised him? Explain in detail why you believe your advice is sound.

4. Lydia Amy, St. Thomas University's dean of enrollment management, believes this problem is "a reflection of people graduating from high school." If she's correct, why do you think fewer males are graduating from high school? Have you witnessed a difference between how males and females approach high school or college? Or have you seen men and women treated differently in these settings? Does anything you've experienced or witnessed seem relevant to this trend?

5. Research the enrollment trends at your school. Are enrollment management professionals concerned about the trends they see? Are measures being taken to improve or maintain diversity on your campus? Do you see having a diverse student body as an important facet of college life? Why or why not?

MAKING IT MATTER

If you have a job while attending school, do you consider yourself a professional taking some courses or a college student who needs to make some money while studying? How do you think this perception of yourself affects your identity as a student?

BREAKING IT DOWN

This article makes an argument by using a cause-and-effect structure. It also uses rhetorical questions to help the reader advance from one point to another. Consider the effectiveness of these choices as you read.

Earning and Learning: Are Students Working Too Much?
MARTIN KRAMER

Martin Kramer is the editor-in-chief of the educational journal New Directions for Higher Education. *He is also an education consultant and former director for Higher Education Planning, U.S. Department of Health, Education and Welfare. This article was originally published in* Change: The Magazine of Higher Learning.

◆

Against the grain of the tradition that honors working your way through college, we should be asking whether students are not working too much. The relative decline of grant funding for student aid as against loans is notorious, but an increased dependence on earnings is important, too.

Part of the increase, of course, reflects the increasing numbers of non-traditional students, who have always typically depended heavily on their own earnings. However, the College Board reports that three-quarters of young, full-time, dependent students held down jobs in 1989–90. Thirty percent of such traditional students had full-time jobs. (These percentages are for students who worked full- or part-time for more than the standard three-month summer vacation. If those students who worked only during the vacation are also counted, the percentages are considerably higher, but possibly irrelevant to this article.)

What no one can quite tell us is why students work so much. Part of the explanation is easy, but only a part. College costs, especially (but not solely) tuition, have risen much faster than real wages in the kinds of jobs students are likely to get, so it takes more hours of work to cover even a constant percentage of costs. But aid offices often have had less grant money to award relative to rising costs. So the aid offices expect students to cover a larger percentage of their budgets through earnings (and loans) to meet expectations of "self-help." Thus, the proportion of all financial "aid" taking the form of such self-help increased from 31 percent in the 1972–73 academic year to 51 percent by 1991–92.

It is not, however, quite as simple as this. Some students deal with the self-help dilemma by working more because they want to borrow less. Loan aversion has almost certainly diminished importantly, but there are still women who want to avoid a "negative dowry" of debt, and there are still first-generation college students who are sufficiently uncertain of their ability to complete degrees and find good jobs afterward that the idea of debt—at least large amounts of debt—is terrifying. This can make long hours of work in awful jobs look relatively attractive. We don't know the importance of such considerations.

A further complication is that a good many students probably work more, not for such reasons of prudence, but out of sheer hedonism. A job, even one that is not very attractive, can often enable a student to afford a standard of living well beyond the costs the student aid office recognizes as essential. Only earnings are generally available to meet such excess costs—not aid, not even student loans.

All of this makes some of the College Board's figures seriously puzzling even where they are not at all surprising. The College Board reports that nontraditional students (defined as part-time, independent, or over age 24) are much more likely than traditional students (younger, full-time, and dependent) to work full-time during periods of enrollment: 46 percent worked full-time in 1989–90, compared with the 30 percent of traditional students cited earlier. This is not surprising. The puzzle is to know how many students have chosen the non-traditional, part-time route precisely so that they will be able to work full-time. And of these, how many would rather be full-time students—that is, have chosen the nontraditional route not for hedonistic reasons but just to get by?

But, then, you can ask, why should we care? Here we must think about what work means and what education means and what are the potential conflicts between the two. Work, whether for money or not, is one of the eternal subjects of ambivalence in human life. We love it and we hate it. Actually, this is exactly why it is so valuable: work is what you resolve to do when you get up in the morning, whether on a particular day you feel like it or not. This makes it an indispensable rudder in our lives. Work for money is also an anchor: it connects us with the economic concerns of almost everyone, everywhere.

Work is, therefore, something we wish students to have experienced, to learn from and value. Yet work is something they can have too much of. How much is too much, and why, depends a good deal on an individual's stage in the life cycle. For example, a full-time job may be too much for an 18-year-old full-time student but not for an older part-time student who has worked full time for years in a job related to his studies.

Just how is it that work can be too much? Consider, on a purely mundane level, what substantial work obligations do to a student's time. The present generation of students can surely be labeled the over-scheduled generation, and not only those who are nontraditional. They have appointment books that must be checked whenever there is a matter of "fitting in" an activity. Consider some of the things students with substantial work obligations may not be able to "fit in": study groups (unless they will efficiently prepare curricular activities . . .), and peripheral reading (for example, reading not strictly required in preparation for term papers).

Indeed, there is a widespread impression that reading in general is suffering. Many students seem to do practically no unassigned reading. The lists of campus best-sellers sound like the escapist reading of war-weary soldiers in the trenches, not the reading of young people eagerly exploring their culture. I once asked a group of people why the needs of multiculturalism could not be met in important part by adding texts rather than substituting new ones for old ones. A professor at a highly selective university (no dyslexics need apply) responded with apparent shock. He could not conceive of faculty asking students to read 50 more pages a week, let alone 100. To do so would violate the "basic covenant between faculty and students" (as I remember his words).

If reading goes by the board, can thinking be far behind? I remember that in my first full-time, non-academic job I would come across some interesting idea and then would find myself saying, "I'll think about that next weekend." Such deferrals of thought must be commonplace among the overscheduled generation.

Faculty members need not only to value reading and thinking but also to insist that having time to read and think is indispensable to an educational process. Work is therefore too important an issue to be left to the student aid administrators. This is not because they are insensitive to the dimensions of the issue. To the contrary, talk to student aid administrators and you will hear a full range of anecdotes, sensitively described, about what work has meant, positively and negatively, to the growth and success of the students with whom they do business. But student aid administration is a can-do profession. If an institution's budget deliberations result in a tuition increase, then the student aid office will resolutely set about enabling as many students as possible to pay the increase. If that means larger self-help expectations—more loans or work or both—the aid administrators will carry out the policy.

The faculty members whose raises are paid for out of such a tuition increase will rarely make the connection between these facts and their concerns as teachers. They need to. In a highly informative article on this subject in the September/October 1988 issue of *Change*, Anne-Marie McCartan examines how some institutions and individual faculty have adapted to the heavier non-academic workloads of students. She cites many ways colleges can make work more educationally rewarding. It is certainly plausible that 15 to 20 hours of work can be so redeemed. But 30 or 40 hours?

Questions for Writing and Discussion

1. Kramer writes about students attending college in the early 1990s as members of the "overscheduled generation." Does your life ever feel like it's "overscheduled"? If so, what—if anything—could be done to provide you with more unscheduled time? If not, what allows you to maintain a manageable schedule?

2. List some of the effects that Kramer cites as a result of how much students are working while they attend college. Choose one of these effects that you find particularly accurate or particularly inaccurate and write an essay in which you demonstrate, with examples from your own experience, how working too much brings about this result.

3. Whom or what does Kramer blame for the problem of students working too much? Based on your experience as a college student, how valid are Kramer's indictments?

4. One of Kramer's concerns is that reading and thinking suffer as a result of students being "overscheduled." Do you see this as a reality in your life or in the lives of your fellow students? Explain.

Making Connections

1. A number of selections in Chapter Two suggest that students sometimes get mixed messages about such things as sexuality, drinking, and the value of education. Discuss an issue about which you have gotten "mixed messages." Describe those messages and where they've come from, as well as how you've come to develop your own point of view about this issue. You may select one of the topics covered in this chapter or another topic that is meaningful to you.

2. Steven Tesich ("Focusing on Friends") and Meghan Daum ("We're Lying: Safe Sex and White Lies in the Time of AIDS") write personal narratives that rely on honesty and introspection to make points that are relevant and relatable for others. Share a story from your own life that you think might be useful or meaningful to other people because of the unique insight you have about the situation or about yourself.

3. Rebecca Dince ("Could Your Facebook Profile Throw a Wrench in Your Future?"), Mindy Sink ("Drinking Deaths Draw Attention to Old Campus

Problem"), Erin Mallants Rodriguez ("Universities Seeing a Gender Gap in Enrollments"), and Martin Kramer ("Earning and Learning") write about recent or current trends on college campuses. Identify another trend that you notice on your campus and write an article that explores this issue through the use of statistics, interviews, and expert testimony. Consider submitting your article for publication to your college's or local community's newspaper.

Exploring the Web

How to Make Friends at College

http://www.collegeanduniversity.net/collegeinfo/index.cfm?catid=17&pageid=2060&affid=175

Written by Jessica Smith, a student at Indiana University Bloomington, this article gives specific tips about how to find and make friends at college.

Facebook.com

http://www.facebook.com

Facebook.com is one of many social networking sites where people "connect with friends, share interests, join groups, send messages, writes notes and post photos."

Aids Action Committee

http://www.aac.org/

The official website of the Aids Action Committee, this site provides information on preventing and treating HIV/AIDS as well as how to access advocacy and health services for those living with AIDS.

"Some Abstinence Programs Mislead Teens, Report Says"

http://www.washingtonpost.com/wp-dyn/articles/A26623-2004Dec1.html

In this article by Ceci Connolly, posted on Thursday, December 2, 2004, on Washingtonpost.doc, the author reports on a congressional staff analysis that studied over a dozen federally funded abstinence-only sex education programs.

"HIV/AIDS Education in Teacher Preparation Programs"

http://www.ericdigests.org/1997-3/hiv.html
This article by Danielle Skripak and Liane Summerfield argues that
  children should receive HIV/AIDs education no later than
  seventh grade and provides resources to assist elementary
  and middle school teachers in developing comprehensive, age-
  appropriate curricula about this public health concern.

Alcohol and College Students

http://alcoholism.about.com/od/college/
This site provides a collection of articles compiled by About.com relevant to alcohol use and college students.

"Population Reference Bureau: Recent U.S. Graduates Choose College"

*http://www.prb.org/AmeristatTemplate.cfm?Section=Education1&templ
  ate=/ContentManagement/ContentDisplay.cfm&ContentID=7851*
This document presents statistical information about trends for college enrollment. The site itself, sponsored by the Population
  Reference Bureau, provides a large volume of statistical reports
  from a number of nonprofit organizations, including Ameristat
  and the Center for Public Information on Population Research.

"U.S. Census Bureau: School Enrollment"

http://www.census.gov/population/www/pop-profile/schenrol.html
This article by Rosalind R. Bruno looks at studies done by the U.S.
  Census Bureau on school enrollment.

CHAPTER 3

Who's In Charge Here?: Exploring Self-Awareness and Personal Responsibility

Overview

Most college students will admit that there are times when it feels like forces beyond their control are creating unanticipated obstacles. These forces may include such things as a challenging professor, a hard-to-get-along-with roommate or classmate, a noisy neighbor, or a heavier workload than expected. Can you relate to issues like this getting in your way?

Some of these forces may seem to have little to do with college, but everything to do with your ability to make the most of your experience there. They may include a full or part-time job, family responsibilities, social obligations, poor time management skills, low-self-esteem, or even issues that might be more traditionally considered disabilities.

Though these challenges are real, they need not detract from your college experience. Ultimately, the power these forces will have over your life as a college student has more to do with your attitude, habits, priorities, and choices than anything else. As you read this chapter, think about ways that you can get the most out of your experience while being realistic about what it means for you to be a college student.

MAKING IT MATTER

What do you know about learning disabilities or those who have them? Is your knowledge based on personal experience, things you've heard or read, or things you've just assumed? Jot down a list of characteristics or comments that come to mind and where they originate from. After you read this essay, see how they compare to this writer's understanding of one learning disability, attention deficit hyperactivity disorder.

BREAKING IT DOWN

Although Gilbert's primary strategy for developing her essay is definition, she also employs illustration, description, narration, and cause and effect. Can you identify where in her essay she is using each of these secondary strategies?

ADHD: The Cloud Lifted

JULIE GILBERT

Julie Gilbert is a student at Bristol Community College studying computer information systems. She is on the Dean's List and intends to use her interest in computer technology to create programs that will accommodate students with ADHD.

———————— ✦ ————————

I'll never forget sitting in the child psychology ward of Floating Hospital in Boston. I was ten. I remember thinking that these people were fools. There was nothing wrong with me. There was no problem. The problem was that the rest of the world didn't agree. I overheard the doctor telling my mother that, while I scored above genius level for intelligence, I had a learning disorder called Attention Deficit Hyperactivity Disorder. He told my mother that it was a recently discovered disorder, and that it was most likely a chemical imbalance. He recommended a new drug called Ritalin to fix the problem. Even though it was new, ADHD was quickly becoming a stigma to label kids that didn't act right. ADHD was, and still is, considered to be an epidemic of badly behaving kids that can't pay attention in class. To them, we were bad learners, bad influences and lost causes. To us, we were smart, different, overmedicated and misunderstood.

As a kid, I always had excellent grades, but I was always being sent to the principal's office. In fact, I was there so often, the principal made me my very own desk right next to his. I wasn't a bad kid. I wasn't misbehaving. I just had too much energy for the rest of the class. They said I had "ants in my pants" and that I was daydreaming and sometimes disruptive. They labeled me as a problem child and said I needed "extra help" in a little classroom isolated on the third floor of St. Michael's School in Swansea. I remember thinking, "This isn't extra help. We're playing board games and solving puzzles." This was my first experience with the "special needs" program.

As I started to grow up, my grades went down. In sixth grade, it was all my mother could handle. That's when the school recommended I get tested for ADHD and that's when I became a permanent part of the Special Education Program. I spent years in small rooms on a wide array of medications. I spent day after day with kids that had various learning disorders such as Down syndrome and other sometimes-severe cases of retardation. When I questioned why I was there, I was told that I was no better than any of them. Other kids would make fun of me horribly and relentlessly. They said that I was too stupid to do my homework. I had very few friends and I started to believe I was retarded. I started thinking that I was going to end up as a drooling, overmedicated lady in a home for society's leftovers. Yet, I still dreamt of college.

I was sixteen years old the day I walked into the guidance office at school. I knew I couldn't afford college on my own. I was worried that I may never get the chance to get a degree and that I was going to be stuck working retail for the rest of my life. I remember feeling sincere when I asked my guidance counselor for her help with finding scholarships or other forms of financial aid. To this day, I can still hear her reply as clear as the day she said it. "Oh, don't even bother Julie. You won't even get accepted." The truth is her statement was a mirror for how every other teacher viewed me. I was never even given the chance to be normal. People stopped talking to me, and asking me what was wrong. Instead they made excuses for why I acted the way I did.

I started looking into the military as an alternate lifestyle. However, when I started testing for job placement in the Air Force, something amazing started to happen. Every test I took, I aced. On the entrance test, where the average score was 50, I scored an 86. On the test to determine linguistic aptitude, where the normal score was a failure of 30, I scored a 99. Recruiters from all of the branches began to fight for my signature. Before too long, I was on my way to the Defense Language Institute in Monterey, CA, to become a Crypto Linguistics Analyst. Finally, after four years, I realized I wasn't retarded after all.

I started researching ADHD. I came across a book. It was called, "Attention Deficit Disorder: A Different Perception," by Thom Hartmann. What I read changed the way I looked at everything, but mainly about myself. In it the author suggested that it wasn't a disorder at all. He suggested that "ADHD" people merely required a different skill set for learning. He spelled out how evolution, not environment, was the most convincing cause. He used the analogy of the hunter in the gatherer's world. Most kids that have ADHD also have above genius intelligence. He argued that they aren't inattentive at all. They are just bored. They learn at such an accelerated pace that most teachers simply can't keep up. They have incredible talents creatively and artistically.

He was right. At least for me, he was. I had spent so much of my existence in a dark cloud, surrounded by thick walls that made me feel closed off from everyone else. I started to realize that I wasn't subnormal. I was different, and different didn't mean bad. I started to embrace my skill set and discover how to use it to learn. I literally had to relearn everything in a way that made sense to me. I see things so much clearer now. I decided to go back to school a few years ago with no firm plan on a course of study. I just took classes that I thought might interest me. After two years, I now have over twenty-four credits with a 3.8 GPA. I am currently enrolled in a computer science program and am considering MIT to complete my B.S. in Programming. I'm studying to learn how to code the game engines for video games. On April 1, 2005, I will be inducted into the National Honor Society, a feat I never before thought I was capable of. I think about all the other kids that are going through what I went through and I wonder if they'll ever feel as confident as I do. The world still overmedicates a lot of them and hides them in tiny rooms. They are still misunderstood. I often wonder if the world will ever realize how gifted and intelligent they really are.

Questions for Writing and Discussion

1. Gilbert uses her own experience to educate people about how the reality of ADHD differs from common misconceptions of the disorder. Using Gilbert's work as a model, write an essay that sheds light on a condition, social issue, or stereotype that you have firsthand knowledge about. Like this essay, your piece should present a more accurate view of this issue than the way it is typically depicted.

2. Consider the way that this essay opens. Do you think it's an effective and appropriate way to grab the reader's attention? Why or why not?

3. One of the ways that Gilbert's school tried to accommodate her ADHD was to assign her to special education classes. Consider the author's experience and do some additional research on how special education programs function in elementary, middle, and high schools. Explore the difference between the mainstreaming or inclusion model and the model that Gilbert's school used. Based on this essay and on your research, which model(s) do you think are most effective?

4. The author of this essay writes that she "had to relearn everything in a way that made sense to [her]." College students with disabilities realize that after high school it becomes their responsibility to seek out the appropriate accommodations for their particular learning styles. Visit the office of disability services at your college and find out what a student with a disability needs to do to secure accommodations or get help advocating for him- or herself at your school. Did you learn anything that surprised you? Explain.

MAKING IT MATTER

Have you ever taken or considered taking a distance learning course? What do you suspect are the benefits of this type of educational experience? What about the pitfalls?

BREAKING IT DOWN

Consider Jodi Morse's introduction. Why do you think this type of introduction is effective for an article such as this? How might Morse's audience and point of view have impacted her decision to open her article this way?

Log On to Learn
JODI MORSE

Jodi Morse, an award-winning education journalist, wrote this article for Time Digital: Supplement to TIME Magazine *in 2000.*

———————— ✦ ————————

I always dreaded the first day of school. My parents like to remind me that I spent the first day of the first grade in denial, making repeated trips back to my kindergarten classroom. On the first day of my junior year in high school, after a summer of endless lobbying to be allowed to drive myself to school, I found myself in the parking lot talking to AAA when I locked my keys in the car with the engine running. During my first day at college, I got lost while looking for a premed placement test and wound up in a cemetery adjacent to the science complex. I took this as a glaring sign and dropped my medical aspirations, promptly enrolling in as many literature courses as possible.

So it was something of a relief to attend the first lecture of English XB17, a survey course of Shakespeare's major plays offered by the University of California, Berkeley's extension program. Other than the short commute from my bed to the laptop at the other end of my 500-sq. ft. studio apartment, no travel was necessary. To find my actual classroom, I simply clicked onto an area of AOL that Berkeley used, where I'd been preregistered, to read and complete my first assignment. And when I worried that I was wasting a sunny July Saturday immersed in an introduction to social and cultural *mores* of the *English Renaissance*. I just stepped outside for a walk. Then I returned to my desk, leisurely phoned a friend and settled down to work.

I quickly learned why so many Americans are heading off to college without leaving their keyboards. They're logging on to sites set up by prestigious schools like Berkeley, Columbia and Stanford, as well as to a new breed of *cyber-only* institutions, such as Jones International University and Western Governors University. Online learning is especially appealing at a time when traditional college students—those 18- to 22-year-olds who spend four years living on campus and attending classes and key parties—make up just 16% of total university enrollment. The vast majority of today's students are time-crunched adults who must pencil in college diplomas and graduate degrees between hectic jobs and kids' soccer games.

The upshot: during this academic year, some 2 million people will take online classes.

Investors are jumping at the opening. In 1999, online learning accounted for just $1.2 billion of the $249 billion higher-education industry; by 2003 that figure is projected to grow to $7 billion, according to *Merrill Lynch*. With the aid of eager venture capitalists, new *virtual schools* are sprouting up, and the old brick-and-mortar ones are *appending* for-profit Web arms and paying their professors in stock options. Even the U.S. Army has climbed into the online-learning trenches, budgeting $600 million over the next six years to enable recruits to get degrees from U.S. colleges, no matter where they're stationed.

Proponents of online learning predict that such advances will one day render *academe* about as relevant as ancient Greek. They contend that students in online classes get more faculty interaction than those packed into a cavernous lecture hall—and for much less money. And they gush about a not-so-distant scenario in which any student will be able to get higher education on demand and employers will give those online credentials the same stock as an *Ivy League* diploma.

Visions of tumbling *ivory towers* have naturally made many academics *apoplectic*. They fear that professors' livelihoods will be debased by upstart courses, often taught by "instructors" who lack Ph.D.s and work for cut rates. Self-preservation aside, they contend that no amount of technological know-how can approach four years of in-person *pedagogy*. Not to mention four years of priceless collegiate intangibles like late-night philosophizing sessions and first loves. "The real challenge as a teacher is to turn the lights on and get the pot boiling, and you can really only do that face to face," says David Noble, a history professor at Toronto's York University and a persistent critic of online learning. "At these digital diploma mills, all you get is a cyber-counterfeited education."

I decided to conduct an unscientific study of my own and take a class. (I paid my $505 and enrolled like any other student, but at the end of the course I told the professor I was a journalist.) I gravitated to Berkeley mainly because of its reputation, but also because its online courses are still fairly low-tech, requiring nothing more than the 56K modem I have on my laptop at home. And I enjoyed the catchy motto: "Bringing the university to you."

I briefly considered Classics of Children's Literature and History of Film, but I settled on Shakespeare. The description boasted that the course was the "Winner of the 1997 Helen Williams Award for Excellence in Collegiate Independent Study." Whatever that was, I was sold. Plus, as a one-time English major, I'd read more than my share of Shakespeare and felt I had a fairly good basis to judge the quality of the instruction. I also thought my background might enable me to skimp on some of the reading if I got busy. Finally, I could think of no educational experience that better evoked my own undergraduate years than my two semesters of Shakespeare. Once in a while, I still get flashbacks of my Shakespeare professor, an old-fashioned *curmudgeon*, hand to his heart, belting out an impassioned *Hamlet* soliloquy to a *rapt* class.

My online class was of the so-called *asynchronous* variety, meaning that instead of *Convening* at an appointed time each week to learn and discuss material, each student works at his or her own pace. Lectures typically are downloaded from the Internet or, as in my case, arrive in printed form through the mail. Discussions take the form of running commentaries snaking through topical message boards. Students are encouraged to arrange live chat discussions and, *in lieu of* weekly office hours, e-mail their professor whenever questions arise.

While it is a blessing for the eternally overbooked, like me, the asynchronous format did little to foster class unity. After reading each play, we were required to post a response on a message board and take up a question posed by one of our classmates. If a particularly spirited discussion was under way (example: cross-dressing Shakespearean actors), our professor, Mary Ann Koory, would send out an e-mail prodding us to log on. But other than those infrequent nudges, it was left up to us to decide how actively we participated. Asynchronicity was liberating in at least one sense, however. As an undergrad, I detested those class drones who always monopolized the discussion. They're just as *garrulous* and annoying over e-mail, tending to post their observations in loud colors like fire-engine red, but here they're easier to avoid. Just don't click on them.

I'd be hard-pressed to tell anything about my classmates or even how many were in the class at one time, since we were all chugging through the lessons at such varied paces. I'd often find myself responding to a posting by a student who had no intention of returning to that topic—he'd already moved on to the next lesson. And my attempts at starting a live group discussion in our class chat room were equally fruitless; only one other person showed up for my chat on Richard III's villainy. And it was the professor.

The quality of her teaching more than made up for the flat class dynamic. The "lectures" were learned, lively and strewn throughout with entertaining pop-cultural allusions. At one point, we were told to consider Shakespeare's folio of plays as a compilation of the best-ever *Grateful Dead bootlegs*. Mary Ann (we were on a first-name basis from our very first e-mail) says she makes use of current events to connect with the varied backgrounds of her students. Most of the time the technique worked, though I could have done without the essay question asking us to compare and contrast Othello with O.J. Simpson.

The work load, as is often the case in online courses, was much heftier—for both students and professor—than in a typical college course. Here, each reading assignment had an essay of several "screens" followed by a three-hour final. After netting a string of B's and lukewarm comments, I realized my skimp-on-reading strategy wouldn't cut it. Mary Ann perceptively tagged my early work a "little light on the logical argument," noting that "you were more interested in your prose than in Shakespeare's work." After that zinger, I stepped up my scholarship. And though I never took the final, I was pulling A's by the course's end.

Mary Ann's best response time was just one hour after I handed in a paper, and her comments often engendered a string of follow-up e-mails. She says such one-on-one discussions are the norm—she often converses more with her online students than with those taking the in-person version. And those online discussions are often much more inclusive. "For shy people, the social barriers fall away online," she told me. "However *attenuated*, online conversations tend to be of higher quality and much more democratic in the best *Jeffersonian* sense of the word."

Even though my e-mails with Mary Ann were stimulating, I wondered if they would have been enough to keep me enthralled if I hadn't been writing this article. According to some estimates, the dropout rate from some online courses can be as high as 50%, compared with just 26% at traditional schools. "Older students' lives are full of disruptions," says Vicky Phillips, CEO of Geteducated.com, a distance-learning research and consulting firm. "Work responsibilities change, kids get sick, people get divorced." My disruptions were less *Cataclysmic* (cable TV and phone calls), but they often proved urgent enough to pull me off an essay for several hours or days.

Many online proponents are looking to the more cutting-edge technologies, such as live streaming video, to curb online student apathy. Other online programs, like Duke University's well-regarded M.B.A. program, require students to come together for a certain number of in-person classes. But schools without a campus don't have that luxury and must find other ways to gin up school spirit: Jones International University has opened an online school store and sends its students late-night snacks. Kentucky Virtual University is sponsoring a digital football league, and Kaplancollege.com has plans for online yearbooks and weekly mixers.

Class bonding is much less of an obstacle for students who progress through a full-fledged online degree program together. Take Marilyn McKay, a marketing consultant in a two-year online M.B.A. program at the University of Maryland University College. McKay, who has a more than full-time job at her own firm and lives in the isolated California desert, chose online learning for its flexibility. "You really learn much more about people than in one of those crowded 200-person lectures where the professor uses the same notes he has for the past 10 years and no one speaks up," she says. Plus, she reminded me, meeting people in print can sometimes be more revealing than sharing small talk while filing into a classroom. "For starters," she says, "you learn quickly who knows how to spell and who uses bad grammar."

McKay is 53 and has grown children. For serious graduate students like her—or even serious dabblers like me—online learning may work. But for the millions of wide-eyed 18-year-olds out there, it's still no contest. Which may explain why, after putting out calls to some of the major online programs, I could turn up only one student who was awarded an undergraduate diploma online. Tasha Overton, 23, got a B.S. in computer programming last year from University of Maryland University College. The primary interpersonal connections she says she made were in her sorority, which she joined during the semester she spent on campus at Tennessee's Austin Peay State University: "I was interested only in getting through my classes, and I didn't go to college to meet people. For me, online education meant the freedom from ever having to set foot in a classroom."

However, even the staunchest backers of online learning would curtail that freedom. According to Geteducated.com's Phillips, "Colleges will always exist as we know them as social *rites of passage*. People don't only go off to college to learn Plato, but to come of age." And they do so not just by hearing an inspired literary mind render *Hamlet*, but also by spending the first day of class dazed and confused in a field of tombstones.

Questions for Writing and Discussion

1. In her introduction, Morse talks about why she has "always dreaded the first day of school." Describe your first day as a college student. What was your attitude as you prepared for the day? What surprised you? Looking back, do you think your first impressions were accurate? Explain.

2. The author uses a number of strategies to inform her audience about online learning, including personal narrative, statistical evidence, and interviews. Which of these strategies do you find most compelling? Why do you think she's chosen to include the others?

3. Did it surprise you to learn that traditional-age students who live on campus account for only "16% of total university enrollment"? Do you consider yourself part of this minority? What advantages and disadvantages do you think the other 84 percent of college students experience?

4. Make a list of the pros and cons Morse identifies for taking an online course. If you have ever been or are currently enrolled in an online course, compare Morse's list with a list of your own. If you have no experience with online education, interview a student who has taken an online course and compare his or her pros and cons. What similarities do you see? What differences? Based on your research, what, if anything, can you conclude?

MAKING IT MATTER

How do you define academic integrity? What does it mean to plagiarize? Do you feel confident about your understanding of these words? If not, how could you get clarification?

BREAKING IT DOWN

Consider Finkel's choice to break his article into sections with subheadings. Why do you think he made that choice? What effect does it have on you as a reader?

Sticky Fingers on the Information Superhighway
ED FINKEL

Ed Finkel is a Senior Writer for Community College Week, *where this article was originally published in 2005.*

───────────── ✦ ─────────────

Honesty's the best policy. It's an adage that seems as old as time, yet the time seems to have come when academic dishonesty is on the rise among college students writing papers about everything from the Gettysburg Address to the works of Mark Twain, professors say. The biggest reason? The proliferation of information sites—and term-paper mills—online during the past decade. For example, a Google search for the phrase "four score and seven years ago" runs up 7,410 references.

"A majority of students are not cheating, but there is a large minority," said Dr. Stephen Lambert, a writing professor at the Brandon campus of Hillsborough Community College in Tampa, Fla. "I take as evidence that there are so many paper mills online. If students weren't availing themselves of that service, these things would just dry up."

ON THE RISE

More specific evidence comes from Dr. Donald L. McCabe, a professor of management at Rutgers University and the founder of The Center for Academic Integrity at Duke University. His research shows that about 40 percent of students admit to plagiarizing at least "a few sentences to a paragraph" during the past year, although "much lower numbers" say they've downloaded an entire paper.

"The increase in the number of plagiarizers is not that overwhelming." McCabe said, "What's gotten worse is those students who had already made the decision that it's OK to plagiarize have done more of it."

However, McCabe's research also has found that overall, 75 percent of students admit to some form of serious cheating—about one-third of them on tests and about one-half on written assignments.

The percentage of students who say they had cut and pasted material from the Internet rose from 10 percent in 1999 to 41 percent in a 2001 survey, with 68 percent saying it wasn't a serious issue.

"It's on the increase. Definitely. No doubt about that," said Phil Anderson, honors system director at Kansas State University, whose office has jurisdiction over all undergraduate and graduate programs. "Sixty percent of our cases involve some form of plagiarism. A significant percentage of other cases involve unauthorized collaboration."

But Barmak Nassirian, associate executive director of external relations for the American Association of Collegiate Registrars and Admissions Officers, said what the Internet giveth to potential plagiarists, it also taketh away.

"It's gotten easier, as a consequence of which it's gotten, apparently, more frequent," he said. "Having said that, the remedy is the same device. Because obviously the same World Wide Web that enables people to search for commentary on Shakespeare and then paraphrase it, enables the professor to do a similar search and find that."

Professors say the Internet isn't just a technology for today's college students and a top resource—it's also a gateway to a culture based on shared information that lends itself to abuse.

"The Internet is the main driver because it's so easy, it's so accessible," Anderson said. "Every student in the university, if they're asked to research something, the first thing they do is go to the Internet. In many cases the only thing they do is go to the Internet."

This is especially true about the term paper mills, said Nassirian, who remembers similar services being offered on bulletin boards and the backs of matchbooks a generation ago. "Now the same kind of "services" are available on the Internet," he said. "It's a little bit more sophisticated."

WHEREFORE CHEATING?

Students begin downloading papers or, more often, cribbing bits and pieces of text while in high school and, if they're not challenged on it, come to believe there's nothing wrong with this practice, said Dennis Trujillo Johnson, director of counseling and career services at Pueblo Community College in Pueblo, Colo.

"They see the Internet as this body of free information," said Johnson, who also teaches a writing course. Students think that "whatever's on there is theirs. They don't have to cite it. It's public domain. For the most part, a lot of students are just not thinking that they're cheating." But those who download whole papers are deliberately cheating, he said.

Brian McDowell, chair of the journalism department at New York's Morrisville State College, an erstwhile junior college that's transitioning to four-year status, agreed that most students who plagiarize don't realize they're doing it.

"It's kind of a cut-and-paste mentality. With that mentality, intellectual property is the loser," he said. "It's less a conscious effort on their part to plagiarize than it is their understanding that this information is all the world's to use. There's a basic cultural generational misunderstanding by students of what is theirs and what isn't. I'm not saying plagiarism is never intentional."

Students in quantitative classes such as science, mathematics and business are more likely to use other new technologies to cheat on tests than to plagiarize source material from the Internet. Cell phones and PDAs can be used to either store notes for a closed-book test—much as students once wrote answers on the backs of their hands—or for friends to text-message those same answers, much as students once copied off their neighbors.

"It's the modern version of the student who writes down the chemistry equations on the pencils that he or she takes into the classroom," said Jonathan Knight, director of academic freedom and tenure at the American Association of University Professors.

LAYING DOWN THE LAW

Anderson said Kansas State has a committee in place to figure out how to deal with technology's role in cheating. "The technology is certainly an enemy of university integrity, and we have to figure out how to address those issues. The students are on the cutting edge. They know that the cell phone can do a lot more than just make a phone call. I've got faculty members who don't own a cell phone," he added.

Students who live in the dorms at Morrisville State are all issued cell phones rather than land lines, McDowell said. "It has that walkie talkie-like service so you can talk to anybody by hitting a button," he said. "They're banned from class. There's such complete connectedness for our students, on several levels, that it's something you have to be vigilant about as a professor. It's difficult to convince students that they can go without their cell phone and their laptop at times. It's a very stimulated generation."

To alert students who might inadvertently plagiarize due to their lack of understanding of the issue—and to begin to warn those with more nefarious intentions—professors and colleges have become more explicit about their intellectual property policies.

"The best way to fight the problem is if faculty are clear on their expectations on an assignment, and they verbalize it and put it in writing," Anderson said. "Students have to be certain that they understand the parameters of what's expected of them. There's a certain percentage of students who will cheat any opportunity they get. There's a certain percentage of students who will never cheat. And then there's a bunch in the middle.

Knight has seen a clear trend toward upfront policies. "Faculty, perhaps more so than was the case when I began my academic career, are more explicit about expectations with respect to providing papers that are not plagiarized, and also about the potential consequences," he said.

Sharon B. Mills, director of arts and communication and an English professor at Calumet Community College in Morehead City, N.C., said that that's partly because students arrive on campus without values. "Sometimes it takes a long time explaining what is and isn't plagiarism," she said. "Some of the students who come here haven't had to write a research paper in high school. Some of them have had the rules kind of watered down."

Hillsborough's Lambert said he prefers instilling values to instilling fear. "I don't want to encourage them to behave ethically because they're afraid to do something else. I would rather teach them the value of being ethical, the reasons for conducting themselves in an ethical manner," he said.

Another technique professors use is creativity coming up with unusual research topics or writing assignments that involve more synthesis, analysis and personal reflection.

"We've talked to teachers, and (suggested that) the assignment is not, 'Tell me about World War II,'" Trujillo Johnson said. "We try to tailor the assignment so that it's different than the typical assignment. If we get a paper that doesn't quite match that, it's pretty obvious that this is someone else's work."

Professors at Pueblo sometimes ask students to submit drafts of research papers "so we see a progression of the work rather than just an assignment and a finished product," he said.

In assigning literary essays, Mills of Calumet instructs students to weave in their own experiences and not to use secondary sources. After they read *Walden* by Henry David Thoreau, for example, she assigns a paper in which "they have to find 10 quotes that Thoreau says that they think are interesting or intriguing somehow. Then they choose three or four of them and somehow relate them to their own philosophy of life. All of those papers will be different, even if they choose the same quotes."

Faculty at Calumet College of St. Joseph in Whiting, Ind., take a similar approach, said Sister Michele Dvorak, Ed.D., vice president for academic affairs. For example, a professor might ask students to contrast and compare two philosophers and offer their own opinion of the work of each one.

"The student has to do critical thinking to complete that paper. . . The nature of the assignment would suggest that there's less of an opportunity (for cheating)," she said.

BUSTED!

To help detect plagiarism, faculty can require that students submit a writing sample—even just a paragraph or two—on the first day of class, said Angela M. Weller, librarian at Onondaga Community College in Syracuse, N.Y. "They have that on file so they can compare future writing," she said.

An assignment that doesn't square well with a student's other work has been a red flag for Mills. "What is surprising is that students think you won't realize it's plagiarized," she said. "When they get a 50 on the test and then write a perfect paper on Mark Twain, you would think you'd notice it."

The usual first line of defense for faculty is to type suspicious phrases into a search engine such as Google. "Usually you can just tell that it's not their own words," she said. "I went on the Internet and typed in Mark Twain. One paper was exactly there; the other one was pretty close. I printed out the thing and it was like, 'Yep, you caught us.' They were rather embarrassed."

Trujillo Johnson recalled a student writing a paper about "A Day in the Life of Ivan Denisovich" for an assignment in which students had to develop a thesis and back it up with examples. "It just didn't flow well. I went and found three papers that she had taken examples from," he said.

In another, more blatant case, "We had one student who took someone's doctoral dissertation and submitted it as their own work, he said. "It was pretty obvious that it wasn't a community college undergraduate's work."

Faculty at some colleges have turned to anti-plagiarism services like turnitin.com, which advertises that it seeks out and then underlines, color codes and links to copied work anywhere on the Internet in "millions of published works," "tens of thousands of electronic books" and "millions of student papers already submitted."

Lambert said such searches can take seconds, whereas a paper plagiarized from reference books in a library in the pre-Internet era, took all day to detect. "The question is whether the cheating is more prevalent, or whether I'm just dectecting it more," he said.

PAYING THE PRICE

The repercussions for students caught plagiarizing or cheating range from a frank discussion for those who seem to have done it inadvertently—at least initially—to a failing grade on a paper for the first blatant example, to a failing grade for the course or even suspension or expulsion for repeat offenders.

"I don't know of too many institutions that have black-and-white policies where any infraction is grounds for dismissal," Nassirian said. "But generally in those cases where there is a significant breach of ethics, expulsions or suspensions for at least one academic year is the norm. The problem is, where do erroneous quotations or failure to footnote end and plagiarism begin, in a way that can be objectively determined?"

Lambert said he strives to make those distinctions. "If the student, for example, borrowed an idea, one idea, paraphrased in a paper that was 10 pages long, that would be different then the student who downloaded an entire 10-page essay verbatim. I would try to work with the first student. But the second student is obviously attempting to avoid the work altogether. That would be a failing paper," he said.

When students seem sincerely apologetic, Lambert said, he reacts differently then when they deny having cheated. For example, he caught two students who wrote papers for one another, collaborating and changing the wording to make them seem different. "I had a conference with them and they denied it," he said; when they did it again, he had less sympathy.

Calumet's English department usually lets a blatant offender write a paper a second time with a maximum grade of "C," Mills said. "And if he does it again, he would flunk the course," she said.

Trijillo Johnson said Pueblo usually fails the student for the assignment or the class on the first obvious offense and suspends them the second time. But he said he tries not to be confrontational and that students often admit to plagiarizing. "We try to put a face on it, too, that it's not just this big, bad institution that they're trying to trick, but to build a relationship with a student," he said.

To that end, Johnson said, he tries to open students' eyes to the bigger picture. "We'll dialogue on values," he said. "Is this promoting the values that you see yourself wanting to live? (Are these) the values that will help your society and your career? Rather then making it a punishment, we try to use it as a learning experience."

That values-based discussion strikes a chord with Lambert, "Not everyone has a good home life and parents who instill ethics. Not everyone is religious and has that form of ethical training. But everyone goes to school. I don't think we should be moralizers in the classroom. I think we should be models of good ethics I think that's different. I think that's professionalism."

Questions for Writing and Discussion

1. Written for *Community College Week,* this article's primary audience is community college faculty and administration. Write an article on plagiarism for students, citing information from this source and others as needed. Compare your article to this one. Does the focus, tone, or thesis differ? Explain.

2. Do you agree with Brian McDowell that "most students who plagiarize don't know they're doing it," or do you think that Susan B. Mills and Steven Lambert are correct in their belief that some students lack the "values" and "ethics" necessary to avoid cheating? Explain.

3. We've all been tempted to cheat or lie at certain points in our life. Describe a time when you were faced with this temptation. What choice did you make and what, if anything, did you learn from the situation?

4. The final paragraphs of this essay detail plagiarism policies used by some professors. How do these compare with your college's or individual professor's policies? Develop a policy for academic integrity that you think is fair. Your policy should include a definition of terms such as *plagiarism* and *cheating* and state the consequences of violating the policy. Why do you think this policy would be effective?

MAKING IT MATTER

Are you a procrastinator? What tasks are you most likely to put off? How do you cope with this problem?

BREAKING IT DOWN

Graham combines three rhetorical modes (classification, causal analysis, and definition) to make his point. Identify each mode and consider how each contributes to the thesis.

Good and Bad Procrastination
PAUL GRAHAM

Paul Graham is an essayist, programmer, and programming language designer. He is the author of three books: On LISP *(1993),* ANSI Common LISP *(1995) and* Hackers & Painters *(2004). The following selection was originally published at http://www.paulgraham.com/procrastination.html.*

———————————— ✦ ————————————

The most impressive people I know are all terrible procrastinators. So could it be that procrastination isn't always bad?

Most people who write about procrastination write about how to cure it. But this is, strictly speaking, impossible. There are an infinite number of things you could be doing. No matter what you work on, you're not working on everything else. So the question is not how to avoid procrastination, but how to procrastinate well.

There are three variants of procrastination, depending on what you do instead of working on something: you could work on (a) nothing, (b) something less important, or (c) something more important. That last type, I'd argue, is good procrastination.

That's the "absent-minded professor," who forgets to shave, or eat, or even perhaps look where he's going while he's thinking about some interesting question. His mind is absent from the everyday world because it's hard at work in another.

That's the sense in which the most impressive people I know are all procrastinators. They're type-C procrastinators: they put off working on small stuff to work on big stuff.

What's "small stuff?" Roughly, work that has zero chance of being mentioned in your obituary. It's hard to say at the time what will turn out to be your best work (will it be your magnum opus on Sumerian temple architecture, or the detective thriller you wrote under a pseudonym?), but there's a whole class of tasks you can safely rule out: shaving, doing your laundry, cleaning the house, writing thank-you notes—anything that might be called an errand.

Good procrastination is avoiding errands to do real work.

Good in a sense, at least. The people who want you to do the errands won't think it's good. But you probably have to annoy them if you want to get anything done. The mildest seeming people, if they want to do real work, all have a certain degree of ruthlessness when it comes to avoiding errands.

Some errands, like replying to letters, go away if you ignore them (perhaps taking friends with them). Others, like mowing the lawn, or filing tax returns, only get worse if you put them off. In principle it shouldn't work to put off the second kind of errand. You're going to have to do whatever it is eventually. Why not (as past-due notices are always saying) do it now?

The reason it pays to put off even those errands is that real work needs two things errands don't: big chunks of time, and the right mood. If you get inspired by some project, it can be a net win to blow off everything you were supposed to do for the next few days to work on it. Yes, those errands may cost you more time when you finally get around to them. But if you get a lot done during those few days, you will be net more productive.

In fact, it may not be a difference in degree, but a difference in kind. There may be types of work that can only be done in long, uninterrupted stretches, when inspiration hits, rather than dutifully in scheduled little slices. Empirically it seems to be so. When I think of the people I know who've done great things, I don't imagine them dutifully crossing items off to-do lists. I imagine them sneaking off to work on some new idea.

Conversely, forcing someone to perform errands synchronously is bound to limit their productivity. The cost of an interruption is not just the time it takes, but that it breaks the time on either side in half. You probably only have to interrupt someone a couple times a day before they're unable to work on hard problems at all.

I've wondered a lot about why startups are most productive at the very beginning, when they're just a couple guys in an apartment. The main reason may be that there's no one to interrupt them yet. In theory it's good when the founders finally get enough money to hire people to do some of the work for them. But it may be better to be overworked than interrupted. Once you dilute a startup with ordinary office workers—with type-B procrastinators—the whole company starts to resonate at their frequency. They're interrupt-driven, and soon you are too.

Errands are so effective at killing great projects that a lot of people use them for that purpose. Someone who has decided to write a novel, for example, will suddenly find that the house needs cleaning. People who fail to write novels don't do it by sitting in front of a blank page for days without writing anything. They do it by feeding the cat, going out to buy something they need for their apartment, meeting a friend for coffee, checking email. "I don't have time to work," they say. And they don't; they've made sure of that.

(There's also a variant where one has no place to work. The cure is to visit the places where famous people worked, and see how unsuitable they were.)

I've used both these excuses at one time or another. I've learned a lot of tricks for making myself work over the last 20 years, but even now I don't win consistently. Some days I get real work done. Other days are eaten up by errands. And I know it's usually my fault: I *let* errands eat up the day, to avoid facing some hard problem.

The most dangerous form of procrastination is unacknowledged type-B procrastination, because it doesn't feel like procrastination. You're "getting things done." Just the wrong things.

Any advice about procrastination that concentrates on crossing things off your to-do list is not only incomplete, but positively misleading, if it doesn't consider the possibility that the to-do list is itself a form of type-B procrastination. In fact, possibility is too weak a word. Nearly everyone's is. Unless you're working on the biggest things you could be working on, you're type-B procrastinating, no matter how much you're getting done.

In his famous essay You and Your Research (which I recommend to anyone ambitious, no matter what they're working on), Richard Hamming suggests that you ask yourself three questions:

1. What are the most important problems in your field?
2. Are you working on one of them?
3. Why not?

Hamming was at Bell Labs when he started asking such questions. In principle anyone there ought to have been able to work on the most important problems in their field. Perhaps not everyone can make an equally dramatic mark on the world; I don't know; but whatever your capacities, there are projects that stretch them. So Hamming's exercise can be generalized to:

What's the best thing you could be working on, and why aren't you?

Most people will shy away from this question. I shy away from it myself; I see it there on the page and quickly move on to the next sentence. Hamming used to go around actually asking people this, and it didn't make him popular. But it's a question anyone ambitious should face.

The trouble is, you may end up hooking a very big fish with this bait. To do good work, you need to do more than find good projects. Once you've found them, you have to get yourself to work on them, and that can be hard. The bigger the problem, the harder it is to get yourself to work on it.

Of course, the main reason people find it difficult to work on a particular problem is that they don't enjoy it. When you're young, especially, you often find yourself working on stuff you don't really like—because it seems impressive, for example, or because you've been assigned to work on it. Most grad students are stuck working on big problems they don't really like, and grad school is thus synonymous with procrastination.

But even when you like what you're working on, it's easier to get yourself to work on small problems than big ones. Why? Why is it so hard to work on big problems? One reason is that you may not get any reward in the forseeable future. If you work on something you can finish in a day or two, you can expect to have a nice feeling of accomplishment fairly soon. If the reward is indefinitely far in the future, it seems less real.

Another reason people don't work on big projects is, ironically, fear of wasting time. What if they fail? Then all the time they spent on it will be wasted. (In fact it probably won't be, because work on hard projects almost always leads somewhere.)

But the trouble with big problems can't be just that they promise no immediate reward and might cause you to waste a lot of time. If that were all, they'd be no worse than going to visit your in-laws. There's more to it than that. Big problems are *terrifying*. There's an almost physical pain in facing them. It's like having a vacuum cleaner hooked up to your imagination. All your initial ideas get sucked out immediately, and you don't have any more, and yet the vacuum cleaner is still sucking.

You can't look a big problem too directly in the eye. You have to approach it somewhat obliquely. But you have to adjust the angle just right: you have to be facing the big problem directly enough that you catch some of the excitement radiating from it, but not so much that it paralyzes you. You can tighten the angle once you get going, just as a sailboat can sail closer to the wind once it gets underway.

If you want to work on big things, you seem to have to trick yourself into doing it. You have to work on small things that could grow into big things, or work on successively larger things, or split the moral load with collaborators. It's not a sign of weakness to depend on such tricks. The very best work has been done this way.

When I talk to people who've managed to make themselves work on big things, I find that all blow off errands, and all feel guilty about it. I don't think they should feel guilty. There's more to do than anyone could. So someone doing the best work they can is inevitably going to leave a lot of errands undone. It seems a mistake to feel bad about that.

I think the way to "solve" the problem of procrastination is to let delight pull you instead of making a to-do list push you. Work on an ambitious project you really enjoy, and sail as close to the wind as you can, and you"ll leave the right things undone.

Questions for Writing and Discussion

1. Rather than providing advice about how not to procrastinate, Graham offers some guidance on how to do it well. In your own words, how would you summarize Graham's advice? Do you agree with Graham? Why or why not?

2. Ask yourself and several other people the following question, "What's the best thing you could be working on, and why aren't you?" Do you notice any similarities in the answers you get? What conclusions, if any, can you draw about procrastination or human nature based on the responses you collected?

3. Graham classifies procrastinators (type A, B, and C) to make his point. Write an essay that classifies successful college students in order to make a point. You might classify them in terms of how, why, or in what ways they are successful. Use specific examples from your experience to develop your essay.

4. Discuss a situation in which you procrastinated because you feared failure. What was the outcome? Since this occurred, have you developed new strategies that help you overcome fear or procrastination? If so, describe them and how they work for you.

5. Using the final portion of Graham's essay as a model, write an essay that highlights the effects of procrastination rather than the causes. Use your experience and that of people you know to support your points.

MAKING IT MATTER

In what ways do you feel that your life outside the classroom differs from the lives of most students you come in contact with? What are the benefits that this difference presents? What are the challenges?

BREAKING IT DOWN

Barbuto offers specific advice to a specific audience. Where could you imagine an article like this being published? Why?

From Single Mother to Successful Student

DANIELLE BARBUTO

Danielle Barbuto is a college student and the mother of an active two-year-old son. She plans to pursue a career in criminal justice after obtaining her associate's degree.

———————— ✦ ————————

A re you a single mother planning to attend college full time and work a part-time job? Hold on tight because your life is about to get crazy. I attend Bristol Community College full time, have a part time job, and am a full-time single mother of a fifteen-month-old boy.

A typical day in my life is probably close to a majority of single mother's. I can become stressed out in the first hour after I awake from a restful sleep. At times, it can be like I'm living my life on fast forward. I'm running in one direction while my son, Anthony, is running in the other. While I am getting breakfast ready for him, he is working hard at finding a good hiding spot for my car keys. Since he's only fifteen months old, you can be sure that he can't tell me that secret hiding spot afterwards. By the time I find my keys, I'm in more of a rush than ever. Once I drop Anthony off at daycare, I'm on my way to a full day of classes. You might think I would be able to enjoy the beautiful scenery on the way to class and relax, but I don't because my brain is going way too fast: did I shut off the lights, did I remember to lock the door, did I pay that bill, and last but not least, did I put all my work in my backpack? With all that stress before class, I wonder if I will even be able to make it through the day, but then again that's what makes me stronger.

After a day at school, I pick up Anthony and rush home to get his night bag ready for the babysitters, so that I can go to work for a few hours. My day is almost done.

Days that I have school and work, I miss my son a lot. I try to make sure on the days I don't work, my time is well spent taking my son to the park or having a good game of hide and go seek.

After work is over, all I have to do is pick up my son and get him ready for bed. This may sound easy enough, but when you're doing it on your own, there is a lot involved in putting a child to bed. In my case, I pick up Anthony's room a little, pick out his clothes for the following day, give him a bath, brush his teeth and put him to bed. Then I make his lunch and anticipate sitting down to relax.

Often, imagining sitting down to relax is as close as I get. The reality is that I will sit at my desk and work on school assignments that are due. After that, I can get my own things ready for the next day. Most nights I feel as if I am asleep before my head even hits the pillow.

I am not whining or complaining for one minute because this is what I have to do as a single mom in order to have a better life for my son and me. If you are in a similar situation, you understand how hectic life can be. So, here are some tips to make life a little easier, and help make you a more successful college student.

First, you have to make sure you are organized at home, at work, at school, and even in your car. If you have one thing out of place, it can end up like a game of Jenga. Pull one block out and everything will collide and crash. Believe me, this was a lot easier to write about than to accomplish. If your home is organized, you will feel a lot better about sitting down to study. I know it is difficult keeping your house clean and organized with a busy schedule and a child to care for, no matter what age they are. As for me, I try hard not to be a clutter bug. Try not to hang on to things that you don't truly need. Since my son has a toy box in his room and in the living room, picking up his toys at the end of the night is not that big of a chore. It takes less than five minutes in each room to throw all his toys into his toy box. After Anthony is in bed, I tidy up the kitchen and living room because, as mothers we know, it is a lot easier to clean when the little one isn't attached to your right leg. For me, rather than letting the house get out of control, I do a little every night before sitting down to do school work. That way it is not so overwhelming.

Try to get everything for yourself and your child prepared in the evening before you sit down. Everyone knows that the less stress people have, the better they can focus on their school work. Instead of thinking of the things I have to do after my school work is done, or the next morning, I do whatever I can that night, in order for the following morning to be less stressful. The more things I can get done at night, the less I will have to do in the morning. This way, I also don't need to worry about forgetting anything. So, sit down and make a list of little things you can get done at night. But, make sure you don't overload yourself either. You will find a plan that just falls into place for you and you will realize it when you do it without even a thought.

Be organized with your school work, too. For example, have a book bag, as well as notebooks, folders, and binders for each subject. Label everything and find a safe spot to keep your papers. Like many people today, I struggle with learning disabilities. One is Attention Deficit Hyperactivity Disorder (ADHD). So, staying neat and organized is a must for me to be a successful college student. I am the type of person who will put something important in a safe spot, and the following day, I have no idea where that safe spot was exactly. If you're like me consider labeling your notebooks and other materials. You may find this helpful.

The most important thing that helps me is scheduling tutorial and study time into my school day. When you have a child, the best thing for you to do is to utilize the time in between classes. This way you can sit and focus without the little one under foot.

My first semester at college was a little easier for me because I didn't know many people there. As the semester continued, I was making friends and meeting new people. While this made being at school more fun, it also made it more difficult to stay focused. Even though you want to spend time with others, use that time wisely if you want to be successful. Having ADHD, I realize how difficult staying focused is, but I also know how much it helps. So, if you have an hour or two during the day, use it to get tutorial help or go to the library where it is a quiet environment for you to study and use the computers.

I even try to keep my car organized. Once again, this is easier said than done. Did you ever notice if you have a messy car, and you drop or misplace something, it seems like the car just swallows it up? Well, my car does the same thing, and my car's favorite snack is school papers. Along with everything else that is going on in your life, try to keep your car clean also. If you stay organized in every aspect of your life, it does make life less stressful. When I lose my sense of organization, my stress level skyrockets.

Secondly, make time for yourself. This is what gets me through the rough times. For example, one night a week I play volleyball or softball, depending on the season. My "me time" usually revolves around some sort of outdoor activity. I love being outside, and sports are my favorite way to unwind. I feel so good when I am outdoors reading in the beautiful fresh air, getting exercise, and being around people who enjoy the same thing. I truly feel it makes me a better mother and student. If you don't make time for yourself, you can become resentful and depressed, and those two things do not help with motherhood or with learning. I love sports, but, you may have different interests. No matter where your interests lie, find a hobby, get a babysitter and enjoy the time. I would like to caution you, however, do not do something that is tiring and stressful for you. That will defeat the purpose. I learned this from a workshop I attended at my college that focused on "leading a happier life." The instructor taught me the secret of having "me time." As mothers, we do not get much of this, but we need to schedule it in. I wish I had learned this even sooner, but I can tell you that from my experiences it does work. When I get home from a volleyball tournament, I feel refreshed and happy, and I look forward to going back the following week. You need to have things in your life that you can look forward to. Of course, you will be able to watch your son/daughter grow, learn, and become a beautiful adult. You will find that you will also be growing, learning, and becoming the best role model for your child. As you know, that can take years, but you can also have things to look forward to weekly.

Last, but not least, from one mother to another, I need to tell you: don't overdo it; you're not super woman. I know as single mothers we may feel that we need to be, but we aren't. I didn't realize this until my son was about one, and I thought my head was going to explode with all the stress of trying to be a perfect mom. But I decided to take "perfect" out of my vocabulary. No one is perfect! I realize that my son needs a roof over his head, food in his stomach, and lots of love in his heart. As long as I can provide that for him, he will grow to be a healthy and strong man, mentally and physically. The rest I do to make myself a better person to be able to provide all that for my son. I have discovered that I cannot stress myself out about it not happening as quickly as I would like because everything will fall into place. I have also learned not to put too much on my plate, or I will end up getting run down and sick from stress. If that happens, the one that loses out the most is your child. All your child needs is your love and attention.

Questions for Writing and Discussion

1. Do you think the advice the author gives about being a successful student is useful to only single mothers with learning disabilities, or might others benefit? Explain.

2. Develop an essay in which you share tips for being a successful student based on your unique experience. Before you begin, consider the specific characteristics of those in your audience. How will understanding your audience make your essay more effective?

3. In what ways do you feel like you are not a traditional college student? For example, do you have children, a full-time job, or more or less life experience than most of the students in your classes? Does this put you at an advantage or disadvantage over other students? Explain.

4. Barbuto doesn't say much in this essay about the impact her professors, advisors, or classmates have had on her success. Why do you think she's chosen to put the focus of this essay where it is?

MAKING IT MATTER

What motivates you to learn? Do grades, requirements, and deadlines help or hinder your motivation? Do you sometimes feel that you learn more when you are not subject to these aspects of traditional college learning?

BREAKING IT DOWN

The following selection uses the technique of flashback to illustrate its point. What is achieved by opening and closing this selection with information about the author's life during the time he is writing versus including only the story about his time in prison?

Saved

MALCOLM X

Malcolm X (1925–1965) was a black militant leader who articulated concepts of racial pride and black nationalism in the early 1960s. The following selection is taken from his autobiography written with Alex Haley.

✦

Many who today hear me somewhere in person, or on television, or those who read something I've said, will think I went to school far beyond the eighth grade. This impression is due entirely to my prison studies.

It had really begun back in the Charlestown Prison, when Bimbi first made me feel envy of his stock of knowledge. Bimbi had always taken charge of any conversation he was in, and I had tried to emulate him. But every book I picked up had few sentences which didn't contain anywhere from one to nearly all of the words that might as well have been in Chinese. When I just skipped those words, of course, I really ended up with little idea of what the book said. So I had come to the Norfolk Prison Colony still going through only book-reading motions. Pretty soon, I would have quit even these motions, unless I had received the motivation that I did.

I saw that the best thing I could do was get hold of a dictionary—to study, to learn some words. I was lucky enough to reason also that I should try to improve my penmanship. It was sad. I couldn't even write in a straight line. It was both ideas together that moved me to request a dictionary along with some tablets and pencils from the Norfolk Prison Colony school.

I spent two days just riffling uncertainly through the dictionary's pages. I'd never realized so many words existed! I didn't know which words I needed to learn. Finally, to start some kind of action, I began copying.

In my slow, painstaking, ragged handwriting, I copied into my tablet everything printed on that first page, down to the punctuation marks.

I believe it took me a day. Then, aloud, I read back, to myself, everything I'd written on the tablet. Over and over, aloud, to myself, I read my own handwriting.

I woke up the next morning, thinking about those words—immensely proud to realize that not only had I written so much at one time, but I'd written words that I never knew were in the world. Moreover, with a little effort, I also could remember what many of these words meant. I reviewed the words whose meanings I didn't remember. Funny thing, from the dictionary first page right now, that "aardvark" springs to my mind. The dictionary had a picture of it, a long-tailed, long-eared, burrowing African mammal, which lives off termites caught by sticking out its tongue as an anteater does for ants.

I was so fascinated that I went on—I copied the dictionary's next page. And the same experience came when I studied that. With every succeeding page, I also learned of people and places and events from history. Actually the dictionary is like a miniature encyclopedia. Finally the dictionary's A section had filled a whole tablet—and I went on into the B's. That was the way I started copying what eventually became the entire dictionary. It went a lot faster after so much practice helped me to pick up handwriting speed. Between what I wrote in my tablet, and writing letters, during the rest of my time in prison I would guess I wrote a million words.

I suppose it was inevitable that as my word-base broadened, I could for the first time pick up a book and read and now begin to understand what the book was saying. Anyone who has read a great deal can imagine the new world that opened. Let me tell you something: from then until I left that prison, in every free moment I had, if I was not reading in the library, I was reading on my bunk. You couldn't have gotten me out of books with a wedge. Between Mr. Muhammad's teachings, my correspondence, my visitors—usually Ella and Reginald—and my reading of books, months passed without my even thinking about being imprisoned. In fact, up to then, I never had been so truly free in my life. . . .

As you can imagine, especially in a prison where there was heavy emphasis on rehabilitation, an inmate was smiled upon if he demonstrated an unusually intense interest in books. There was a sizable number of well-read inmates, especially the popular debaters. Some were said by many to be practically walking encyclopedias. They were almost celebrities. No university would ask any student to devour literature as I did when this new world opened to me, of being able to read and understand.

I read more in my room than in the library itself. An inmate who was known to read a lot could check out more than the permitted maximum number of books. I preferred reading in the total isolation of my own room.

When I had progressed to really serious reading, every night at about ten P.M. I would be outraged with the "lights out." It always seemed to catch me right in the middle of something engrossing.

Fortunately, right outside my door was a corridor light that cast a glow into my room. The glow was enough to read by, once my eyes adjusted to it. So when "lights out" came, I would sit on the floor where I could continue reading in that glow.

At one-hour intervals the night guards paced past every room. Each time I heard the approaching footsteps, I jumped into bed and feigned sleep. And as soon as the guard passed, I got back out of bed onto the floor area of that light-glow, where I would read for another fifty-eight minutes—until the guard approached again. That went on until three or four every morning. Three or four hours of sleep a night was enough for me. Often in the years in the streets I had slept less than that.

I have often reflected upon the new vistas that reading opened to me. I knew right there in prison that reading had changed forever the course of my life. As I see it today, the ability to read awoke inside me some long dormant craving to be mentally alive. I certainly wasn't seeking any degree, the way a college confers status symbol upon its students. My homemade education gave me, with every additional book that I read, a little bit more sensitivity to the deafness, dumbness, and blindness that was afflicting the black race in America. Not long ago, an English writer telephoned me from London, asking questions. One was, "What's your alma mater?" I told him, "Books." You will never catch me with a free fifteen minutes in which I'm not studying something I feel might be able to help the man. . . .

Every time I catch a plane, I have with me a book that I want to read—and that's a lot of books these days. If I weren't out here every day battling the white man, I could spend the rest of my life reading, just satisfying my curiosity—because you can hardly mention anything I'm not curious about. I don't think anybody ever got more out of going to prison than I did. In fact, prison enabled me to study far more intensively than I would have if my life had gone differently and I had attended some college. I imagine that one of the biggest troubles with colleges is there are too many distractions, too much panty-raiding, fraternities, and boola-boola and all of that. Where else but in prison could I have attacked my ignorance by being able to study intensely sometimes as much as fifteen hours a day?

Questions for Writing and Discussion

1. Malcolm X suggests that curiosity is a great motivation for learning. Choose a topic that you are curious about. How do you go about satisfying your curiosity about this topic? Be specific in terms of what or whom you access for information.

2. Malcolm X decided to copy words from the dictionary as a learning strategy. Describe a strategy that you have found successful in terms of improving your academic skills.

3. Is there someone whom you wanted to emulate because he or she was good at or knowledgeable about something? Describe that person and how he or she inspired you to want to learn.

4. Malcolm X feels that he learned more in prison than most people do in college. Describe a situation in which you felt more motivated to learn outside of the classroom than you sometimes do in the classroom. What aspects of this experience can you apply to your in-class experiences to improve your motivation level in all learning environments?

Making Connections

1. Both Julie Gilbert in "ADHD: A Cloud Lifted" and Malcolm X in "Saved" discuss the transformational power of reading. For Gilbert, she learned a new way to perceive and cope with ADHD. For Malcolm X, reading the dictionary and a number of other books "opened up new vistas" to him. It could be argued that reading made both authors feel less alone and more connected to others. Discuss a situation in which you were transformed in some way by reading. Be specific about what you were reading and how it changed you.

2. Danielle Barbuto ("From Single Mother to Successful Student") and Paul Graham ("Good and Bad Procrastination") both offer their readers advice about time management and motivation. Does one author's essay speak to you more than the other? If so, why? If not, explain why you think both authors have something to offer a student like you.

3. A number of essays in this chapter suggest things you can do to enhance your experience as a college student. Make a list of things you are currently doing well. Write a paragraph or two about why you are successful in these

areas. Then identify a couple of things you'd like to improve on. How can you use the strengths that are leading to success in the first areas to improve the weaker ones?

4. The audience for Jodi Morse's "Log On to Learn" and Martin Kramer's "Earning and Learning" (Chapter Two) are college and university communities, but these pieces differ in terms of which member of these communities each writer is targeting. Determine the intended audience for each of these articles. Cite specific passages from each piece to make your case. How do you think the articles might have been different if each author were writing for the other's audience?

Exploring the Web

Attention Deficit Disorder Resources

http://www. addresources. org/
This educational website is sponsored by Attention Deficit Disorder Resources, a nonprofit organization that educates and serves as a resource for people with ADD and ADHD.

ADHD News

http://www.adhdnews.com/
This site includes articles, information, a message board, and other resources for people with ADHD and their friends and families.

Distance Education Clearinghouse

http://www.uwex.edu/disted/home.html
"The Distance Education Clearinghouse . . . managed and maintained by the University of Wisconsin-Extension . . . is a comprehensive . . . [w]ebsite bringing together distance education information from Wisconsin, national, and international sources." This site lists a variety of other sites that provide general information about distance learning as well as current developments, course offerings, and other useful information for both students and teachers.

What Is Plagiarism?

http://gervaseprograms.georgetown.edu/hc/plagiarism.html
Sponsored by Georgetown University's Honor Council, this page provides a definition of plagiarism, common misconceptions about and rationalizations for plagiarizing, and tips to avoid it.

Purdue University Online Writing Lab: Avoiding Plagiarism

http://owl.english.purdue.edu/handouts/research/r_plagiar.html
This document, complete with examples and exercises, "is designed
   to help writers develop strategies for knowing how to avoid acci-
   dental plagiarism."

"Procrastination"

http://www.mentalhelp.net/psyhelp/chap4/chap4r.htm
This link is part of Chapter Four of a downloadable book called
   Psychological Self-Help by clinical psychologist Clayton E.
   Tucker-Ladd, Ph.D. It resides on the Mental Help Net website,
   which "exists to promote mental health and wellness education
   and advocacy."

"Procrastination"

http://www.sas.calpoly.edu/asc/ssl/procrastination.html
An informative and practical article about procrastination from
   California Polytechnic State University's Academic Skills Center.

SingleMom.com

http://www.singlemom.com/
This site, sponsored by a nonprofit organization of the same name,
   provides a variety of resources for single mothers, including educational, career, and financial aid information.

Malcolm X

http://www.cmgww.com/historic/malcolm/home.php
Operated by CMG Worldwide, this site calls itself the "Official
   Website of Malcolm X."

CHAPTER 4

Learning and Unlearning: Reinventing Yourself as a Learner

Overview

By now, you've probably discovered that what brought you to college and the way you balance your academic schedule, work schedule, and social activities say a lot about who you are as a person. But what do you know about yourself as a learner?

Because so much of what you do as a college student relies on you—not your family, teachers, or peers—you have an opportunity to make the most of your education. One way to do this is to learn as much as you can about what makes and breaks successful college students. Although you may be new to college, you are not new to learning. In fact, you may already be realizing that your approach to learning is changing. This may be the result of advice you are getting from mentors and peers, what you have observed as working or not working for you, and, of course, the attitude you have about what you are learning.

This chapter looks at some challenges you may be facing in developing useful learning strategies. You will be asked to consider how you see yourself as a student and how you came to develop the habits and attitudes you have as well as how you might modify what you are doing and thinking in order to increase your chance for success.

MAKING IT MATTER

How do you define intelligence? Do you think your definition is the commonly held view? Explain.

BREAKING IT DOWN

Consider Gardner's choice to add profiles of famous people to illustrate each of the intelligences he is defining. How does this change the tone of the piece? Do you find it effective? Why or why not?

Multiple Intelligences
HOWARD GARDNER

Howard Gardner is a cognitive and educational psychologist based at Harvard University. He questioned the validity of traditional views of intelligence and IQ testing and developed his own theory of multiple intelligences, which has influenced the way that many educators have reformed their teaching practices and assessment methods. The following selection is excerpted from one of his many works, Multiple Intelligences: The Theory in Practice *(1993).*

———————— ✦ ————————

In a traditional view, intelligence is defined operationally as the ability to answer items on tests of intelligence. The inference from the test scores to some underlying ability is supported by statistical techniques that compare responses of subjects at different ages; the apparent correlation of these test scores across ages and across different tests corroborates the notion that the general faculty of intelligence, *g*, does not change much with age or with training or experience. It is an inborn attribute or faculty of the individual.

Multiple intelligences theory, on the other hand, pluralizes the traditional concept. An intelligence entails the ability to solve problems or fashion products that are of consequence in a particular cultural setting or community. The problem-solving skill allows one to approach a situation in which a goal is to be obtained and to locate the appropriate route to that goal. The creation of a *cultural* product is crucial to such functions as capturing and transmitting knowledge or expressing one's views or feelings. The problems to be solved range from creating an end for a story to anticipating a mating move in chess to repairing a quilt. Products range from scientific theories to musical compositions to successful political campaigns.

MI theory is framed in light of the biological origins of each problem-solving skill. Only those skills that are universal to the human species are treated. Even so, the biological proclivity to participate in a particular form of problem solving must also be coupled with the cultural nurturing of that domain. For example, language, a universal skill, may manifest itself particularly as writing in one culture, as oratory in another culture, and as the secret language of anagrams in a third.

Given the desire of selecting intelligences that are rooted in biology, and that are valued in one or more cultural settings, how does one actually identify an "intelligence"? In coming up with our list, we consulted evidence from several different sources: knowledge about normal development and development in gifted individuals; information about the breakdown of cognitive skills under conditions of brain damage; studies of exceptional populations, including prodigies, idiots savants, and autistic children; data about the evolution of cognition over the millennia; cross-cultural accounts of cognition; psychometric studies, including examinations of correlations among tests; and psychological training studies, particularly measures of transfer and generalization across tasks. Only those candidate intelligences that satisfied all or a majority of the criteria were selected as bona fide intelligences. A more complete discussion of each of these criteria for an "intelligence" and the seven intelligences that have been proposed so far, is found in *Frames of Mind*.[1] This book also considers how the theory might be disproven and compares it to competing theories of intelligence. . . .

An intelligence must also be susceptible to encoding in a symbol system—a culturally contrived system of meaning, which captures and conveys important forms of information. Language, picturing, and mathematics are but three nearly worldwide symbol systems that are necessary for human survival and productivity. The relationship of a candidate intelligence to a human symbol system is no accident. In fact, the existence of a core computational capacity anticipates the existence of a symbol system that exploits that capacity. While it may be possible for an intelligence to proceed without an accompanying symbol system, a primary characteristic

[1]Gardner, H. (1983). *Frames of mind: The theory of multiple intelligences.* New York: Basic Books. [All notes are Gardner's.]

of human intelligence may well be its gravitation toward such an embodiment.

THE SEVEN INTELLIGENCES

Having sketched the characteristics and criteria of an intelligence, we turn now to a brief consideration of each of the seven intelligences. We begin each sketch with a thumbnail biography of a person who demonstrates an unusual facility with that intelligence. These biographies illustrate some of the abilities that are central to the fluent operation of a given intelligence. Although each biography illustrates a particular intelligence, we do not wish to imply that in adulthood intelligences operate in isolation. Indeed, except for abnormal individuals, intelligences always work in concert, and any sophisticated adult role will involve a melding of several of them. Following each biography we survey the various sources of data that support each candidate as an "intelligence."

Musical Intelligence

> When he was three years old, Yehudi Menuhin was smuggled into the San Francisco Orchestra concerts by his parents. The sound of Louis Persinger's violin so entranced the youngster that he insisted on a violin for his birthday and Louis Persinger as his teacher. He got both. By the time he was ten years old, Menuhin was an international performer.[2]

Violinist Yehudi Menuhin's musical intelligence manifested itself even before he had touched a violin or received any musical training. His powerful reaction to that particular sound and his rapid progress on the instrument suggest that he was biologically prepared in some way for that endeavor. In this way evidence from child prodigies supports our claim that there is a biological link to a particular intelligence. Other special populations, such as autistic children who can play a musical instrument beautifully but who cannot speak, underscore the independence of musical intelligence.

A brief consideration of the evidence suggests that musical skill passes the other tests for an intelligence. For example, certain

---

[2]Menuhin, Y. (1977). *Unfinished journey.* New York: Knopf.

parts of the brain play important roles in perception and production of music. These areas are characteristically located in the right hemisphere, although musical skill is not as clearly "localized," or located in a specifiable area, as language. Although the particular susceptibility of musical ability to brain damage depends on the degree of training and other individual differences, there is clear evidence for "amusia" or loss of musical ability.

Music apparently played an important unifying role in Stone Age (Paleolithic) societies. Birdsong provides a link to other species. Evidence from various cultures supports the notion that music is a universal faculty. Studies of infant development suggest that there is a "raw" computational ability in early childhood. Finally, musical notation provides an accessible and lucid symbol system.

In short, evidence to support the interpretation of musical ability as an "intelligence" comes from many different sources. Even though musical skill is not typically considered an intellectual skill like mathematics, it qualifies under our criteria. By definition it deserves consideration; and in view of the data, its inclusion is empirically justified.

Bodily-Kinesthetic Intelligence

> Fifteen-year-old Babe Ruth played third base. During one game his team's pitcher was doing very poorly and Babe loudly criticized him from third base. Brother Mathias, the coach, called out, "Ruth, if you know so much about it, YOU pitch!" Babe was surprised and embarrassed because he had never pitched before, but Brother Mathias insisted. Ruth said later that at the very moment he took the pitcher's mound, he KNEW he was supposed to be a pitcher and that it was "natural" for him to strike people out. Indeed, he went on to become a great major league pitcher (and, of course, attained legendary status as a hitter).[3]

Like Menuhin, Babe Ruth was a child prodigy who recognized his "instrument" immediately upon his first exposure to it. This recognition occurred in advance of formal training.

Control of bodily movement is, of course, localized in the motor cortex, with each hemisphere dominant or controlling bodily

---

[3]Connor, A. (1982). *Voices from Cooperstown.* New York: Collier. (Based on a quotation taken from *The Babe Ruth story,* Babe Ruth & Bob Considine. New York: Dutton, 1948.)

movements on the contra-lateral side. In right-handers, the dominance for such movement is ordinarily found in the left hemisphere. The ability to perform movements when directed to do so can be impaired even in individuals who can perform the same movements reflexively or on a nonvoluntary basis. The existence of specific *apraxia* constitutes one line of evidence for a bodily-kinesthetic intelligence.

The evolution of specialized body movements is of obvious advantage to the species, and in humans this adaptation is extended through the use of tools. Body movement undergoes a clearly defined developmental schedule in children. And there is little question of its universality across cultures. Thus it appears that bodily-kinesthetic "knowledge" satisfies many of the criteria for an intelligence.

The consideration of bodily-kinesthetic knowledge as "problem solving" may be less intuitive. Certainly carrying out a mime sequence or hitting a tennis ball is not solving a mathematical equation. And yet, the ability to use one's body to express an emotion (as in a dance), to play a game (as in a sport), or to create a new product (as in devising an invention) is evidence of the cognitive features of body usage. The specific computations required to solve a particular bodily-kinesthetic *problem*, hitting a tennis ball, are summarized by Tim Gallwey:

> At the moment the ball leaves the server's racket, the brain calculates approximately where it will land and where the racket will intercept it. This calculation includes the initial velocity of the ball, combined with an input for the progressive decrease in velocity and the effect of wind and after the bounce of the ball. Simultaneously, muscle orders are given: not just once, but constantly with refined and updated information. The muscles must cooperate. A movement of the feet occurs, the racket is taken back, the face of the racket kept at a constant angle. Contact is made at a precise point that depends on whether the order was given to hit down the line or cross-court, an order not given until after a split-second analysis of the movement and balance of the opponent.
>
> To return an average serve, you have about one second to do this. To hit the ball at all is remarkable and yet not uncommon. The truth is that everyone who inhabits a human body possesses a remarkable creation.[4]

[4]Gallwey, T. (1976). *Inner tennis.* New York: Random House.

Logical-Mathematical Intelligence

In 1983 Barbara McClintock won the Nobel Prize in medicine or physiology for her work in microbiology. Her intellectual powers of deduction and observation illustrate one form of logical-mathematical intelligence that is often labeled "scientific thinking." One incident is particularly illuminating. While a researcher at Cornell in the 1920s McClintock was faced one day with a problem: while *theory* predicted 50-percent pollen sterility in corn, her research assistant (in the "field") was finding plants that were only 25- to 30-percent sterile. Disturbed by this discrepancy, McClintock left the cornfield and returned to her office where she sat for half an hour, thinking:

> Suddenly I jumped up and ran back to the (corn) field. At the top of the field (the others were still at the bottom) I shouted "Eureka, I have it! I know what the 30% sterility is!". . . They asked me to prove it. I sat down with a paper bag and a pencil and I started from scratch, which I had not done at all in my laboratory. It had all been done so fast; the answer came and I ran. Now I worked it out step by step—it was an intricate series of steps—and I came out with [the same result]. [They] looked at the material and it was exactly as I'd said it was; it worked out exactly as I had diagrammed it. Now, why did I know, without having done it on paper? Why was I so sure?[5]

This anecdote illustrates two essential facts of the logical-mathematical intelligence. First, in the gifted individual, the process of problem solving is often remarkably rapid—the successful scientist copes with many variables at once and creates numerous hypotheses that are each evaluated and then accepted or rejected in turn.

The anecdote also underscores the *nonverbal* nature of the intelligence. A solution to a problem can be constructed *before* it is articulated. In fact, the solution process may be totally invisible, even to the problem solver. This need not imply, however, that discoveries of this sort—the familiar "Aha!" phenomenon—are mysterious, intuitive, or unpredictable. The fact that it happens more frequently to some people (perhaps Nobel Prize winners) suggests the opposite. We interpret this as the work of theological-mathematical intelligence.

[5]Keller, E. (1983). *A feeling for the organism* (p. 104). Salt Lake City: W. H. Freeman.

Along with the companion skill of language, logical-mathematical reasoning provides the principal basis for IQ tests. This form of intelligence has been heavily investigated by traditional psychologists, and it is the archetype of "raw intelligence" or the problem-solving faculty that purportedly cuts across domains. It is perhaps ironic, then, that the actual mechanism by which one arrives at a solution to a logical-mathematical problem is not as yet properly understood.

This intelligence is supported by our empirical criteria as well. Certain areas of the brain are more prominent in mathematical calculation than others. There are idiots savants who perform great feats of calculation even though they remain tragically deficient in most other areas. Child prodigies in mathematics abound. The development of this intelligence in children has been carefully documented by Jean Piaget and other psychologists.

Linguistic Intelligence

> At the age of ten, T. S. Eliot created a magazine called "Fireside" to which he was the sole contributor. In a three-day period during his winter vacation, he created eight complete issues. Each one included poems, adventure stories, a gossip column, and humor. Some of this material survives and it displays the talent of the poet.[6]

As with the logical intelligence, calling linguistic skill an "intelligence" is consistent with the stance of traditional psychology. Linguistic intelligence also passes our empirical tests. For instance, a specific area of the brain, called "Broca's Area," is responsible for the production of grammatical sentences. A person with damage to this area can understand words and sentences quite well but has difficulty putting words together in anything other than the simplest of sentences. At the same time, other thought processes may be entirely unaffected.

The gift of language is universal, and its development in children is strikingly constant across cultures. Even in deaf populations where a manual sign language is not explicitly taught, children will often "invent" their own manual language and use it surreptitiously! We thus see how an intelligence may operate independently of a specific input modality or output channel.

---

[6]Soldo, J. (1982). Jovial juvenilia: T. S. Eliot's first magazine. Biography, 5, 25–37.

Spatial Intelligence

Navigation around the Caroline Islands in the South Seas is accomplished without instruments. The position of the stars, as viewed from various islands, the weather patterns, and water color are the only sign posts. Each journey is broken into a series of segments; and the navigator learns the position of the stars within each of these segments. During the actual trip the navigator must envision mentally a reference island as it passes under a particular star and from that he computes the number of segments completed, the proportion of the trip remaining, and any corrections in heading that are required. The navigator cannot *see* the islands as he sails along; instead he maps their locations in his mental "picture" of the journey.[7]

Spatial problem solving is required for navigation and in the use of the notational system of maps. Other kinds of spatial problem solving are brought to bear in visualizing an object seen from a different angle and in playing chess. The visual arts also employ this intelligence in the use of space.

Evidence from brain research is clear and persuasive. Just as the left hemisphere has, over the course of evolution, been selected as the site of linguistic processing in right-handed persons, the right hemisphere proves to be the site most crucial for spatial processing. Damage to the right posterior regions causes impairment of the ability to find one's way around a site, to recognize faces or scenes, or to notice fine details.

Patients with damage specific to regions of the right hemisphere will attempt to compensate for their spacial deficits with linguistic strategies. They will try to reason aloud, to challenge the task, or even make up answers. But such nonspatial strategies are rarely successful.

Blind populations provide an illustration of the distinction between the spatial intelligence and visual perception. A blind person can recognize shapes by an indirect method: running a hand along the object translates into length of time of movement, which in turn is translated into the size of the object. For the blind person, the perceptual system of the tactile modality parallels the visual modality in the seeing person. The analogy between

[7]Gardner, H. (1983). *Frames of mind: The theory of multiple intelligences.* New York: Basic Books.

the spatial reasoning of the blind and the linguistic reasoning of the deaf is notable.

There are few child prodigies among visual artists, but there are idiots savants such as Nadia.[8] Despite a condition of severe autism, this preschool child made drawings of the most remarkable representational accuracy and finesse.

Interpersonal Intelligence

With little formal training in special education and nearly blind herself, Anne Sullivan began the intimidating task of instructing a blind and deaf seven-year-old Helen Keller. Sullivan's efforts at communication were complicated by the child's emotional struggle with the world around her. At their first meal together, this scene occurred:

> Annie did not allow Helen to put her hand into Annie's plate and take what she wanted, as she had been accustomed to do with her family. It became a test of wills—hand thrust into plate, hand firmly put aside. The family, much upset, left the dining room. Annie locked the door and proceeded to eat her breakfast while Helen lay on the floor kicking and screaming, pushing and pulling at Annie's chair. [After half an hour] Helen went around the table looking for her family. She discovered no one else was there and that bewildered her. Finally, she sat down and began to eat her breakfast, but with her hands. Annie gave her a spoon. Down on the floor it clattered, and the contest of wills began anew.[9]

Anne Sullivan sensitively responded to the child's behavior. She wrote home: "The greatest problem I shall have to solve is how to discipline and control her without breaking her spirit. I shall go rather slowly at first and try to win her love."

In fact, the first "miracle" occurred two weeks later, well before the famous incident at the pumphouse. Annie had taken Helen to a small cottage near the family's house, where they could

---

[8]Selfe, L. (1977). *Nadia: A case of extraordinary drawing in an autistic child.* New York: Academic Press.

[9]Lash, J. (1980). *Helen and teacher: The story of Helen Keller and Anne Sullivan Macy* (p. 52). New York: Delacorte.

live alone. After seven days together, Helen's personality suddenly underwent a profound change—the therapy had worked:

> My heart is singing with joy this morning. A miracle has happened! The wild little creature of two weeks ago has been transformed into a gentle child.[10]

It was just two weeks after this that the first breakthrough in Helen's grasp of language occurred; and from that point on, she progressed with incredible speed. The key to the miracle of language was Anne Sullivan's insight into the *person* of Helen Keller.

Interpersonal intelligence builds on a core capacity to notice distinctions among others; in particular, contrasts in their moods, temperaments, motivations, and intentions. In more advanced forms, this intelligence permits a skilled adult to read the intentions and desires of others, even when these have been hidden. This skill appears in a highly sophisticated form in religious or political leaders, teachers, therapists, and parents. The Helen Keller–Anne Sullivan story suggests that this interpersonal intelligence does not depend on language.

All indices in brain research suggest that the frontal lobes play a prominent role in interpersonal knowledge. Damage in this area can cause profound personality changes while leaving other forms of problem solving unharmed—a person is often "not the same person" after such an injury.

Alzheimer's disease, a form of presenile dementia, appears to attack posterior brain zones with a special ferocity, leaving spatial, logical, and linguistic computations severely impaired. Yet, Alzheimer's patients will often remain well groomed, socially proper, and continually apologetic for their errors. In contrast, Pick's disease, another variety of presenile dementia that is more frontally oriented, entails a rapid loss of social graces.

Biological evidence for interpersonal intelligence encompasses two additional factors often cited as unique to humans. One factor is the prolonged childhood of primates, including the close attachment to the mother. In those cases where the mother is removed from early development, normal interpersonal development is in serious jeopardy. The second factor is the relative importance in humans of social interaction. Skills such as hunting, tracking, and killing in prehistoric societies required participation

---

[10]Lash (p. 54)

and cooperation of large numbers of people. The need for group cohesion, leadership, organization, and solidarity follows naturally from this.

INTRAPERSONAL INTELLIGENCE

In an essay called "A Sketch of the Past," written almost as a diary entry, Virginia Woolf discusses the "cotton wool of existence"— the various mundane events of life. She contrasts this "cotton wool" with three specific and poignant memories from her childhood: a fight with her brother, seeing a particular flower in the garden, and hearing of the suicide of a past visitor.

> These are three instances of exceptional moments. I often tell them over, or rather they come to the surface unexpectedly. But now for the first time I have written them down, and I realize something that I have never realized before. Two of these moments ended in a state of despair. The other ended, on the contrary, in a state of satisfaction.
>
> The sense of horror (in hearing of the suicide) held me powerless. But in the case of the flower, I found a reason; and was thus able to deal with the sensation. I was not powerless.
>
> Though I still have the peculiarity that I receive these sudden shocks, they are now always welcome; after the first surprise, I always feel instantly that they are particularly valuable. And so I go on to suppose that the shock-receiving capacity is what makes me a writer. I hazard the explanation that a shock is at once in my case followed by the desire to explain it. I feel that I have had a blow; but it is not, as I thought as a child, simply a blow from an enemy hidden behind the cotton wool of daily life; it is or will become a revelation of some order; it is a token of some real thing behind appearances; and I make it real by putting it into words.[11]

This quotation vividly illustrates the intrapersonal intelligence—knowledge of the internal aspects of a person: access to one's own feeling life, one's range of emotions, the capacity to effect discriminations among these emotions and eventually to label them and to draw upon them as a means of understanding and

---

[11]Woolf, V. (1976). *Moments of being* (pp. 69–70). Sussex: The University Press.

guiding one's own behavior. A person with good intrapersonal intelligence has a viable and effective model of himself or herself. Since this intelligence is the most private, it requires evidence from language, music, or some other more expressive form of intelligence if the observer is to detect it at work. In the above quotation, for example, linguistic intelligence is drawn upon to convey intrapersonal knowledge; it embodies the interaction of intelligences, a common phenomenon to which we will return later.

We see the familiar criteria at work in the intrapersonal intelligence. As with the interpersonal intelligence, the frontal lobes play a central role in personality change. Injury to the lower area of the frontal lobes is likely to produce irritability or euphoria; while injury to the higher regions is more likely to produce indifference, listlessness, slowness, and apathy—a kind of depressive personality. In such "frontal-lobe" individuals, the other cognitive functions often remain preserved. In contrast, among aphasics who have recovered sufficiently to describe their experiences, we find consistent testimony: while there may have been a diminution of general alertness and considerable depression about the condition, the individual in no way felt himself to be a different person. He recognized his own needs, wants, and desires and tried as best he could to achieve them.

The autistic child is a prototypical example of an individual with impaired intrapersonal intelligence; indeed, the child may not even be able to refer to himself. At the same time, such children often exhibit remarkable abilities in the musical, computational, spatial, or mechanical realms.

Evolutionary evidence for an intrapersonal faculty is more difficult to come by, but we might speculate that the capacity to transcend the satisfaction of instinctual drives is relevant. This becomes increasingly important in a species not perennially involved in the struggle for survival.

In sum, then, both interpersonal and intrapersonal faculties pass the tests of an intelligence. They both feature problem-solving endeavors with significance for the individual and the species. Interpersonal intelligence allows one to understand and work with others; intrapersonal intelligence allows one to understand and work with oneself. In the individual's sense of self, one encounters a melding of inter- and intrapersonal components. Indeed, the sense of self emerges as one of the most marvelous of human inventions—a symbol that represents all kinds of information about a person and that is at the same time an invention that all individuals construct for themselves.

SUMMARY: THE UNIQUE CONTRIBUTIONS OF THE THEORY

As human beings, we all have a repertoire of skills for solving different kinds of problems. Our investigation has begun, therefore, with a consideration of these problems, the contexts they are found in, and the culturally significant products that are the outcome. We have not approached "intelligence" as a reified human faculty that is brought to bear in literally any problem setting; rather, we have begun with the problems that humans *solve* and worked back to the "intelligences" that must be responsible.

Evidence from brain research, human development, evolution, and cross-cultural comparisons was brought to bear in our search for the relevant human intelligences: a candidate was included only if reasonable evidence to support its membership was found across these diverse fields. Again, this tack differs from the traditional one: since no candidate faculty is *necessarily* an intelligence, we could choose on a motivated basis. In the traditional approach to "intelligence," there is no opportunity for this type of empirical decision.

We have also determined that these multiple human faculties, the intelligences, are to a significant extent *independent*. For example, research with brain-damaged adults repeatedly demonstrates that particular faculties can be lost while others are spared. This independence of intelligence implies that a particularly high level of ability in one intelligence, say mathematics, does not require a similarly high level in another intelligence, like language or music. This independence of intelligences contrasts sharply with traditional measures of IQ that find high correlations among test scores. We speculate that the usual correlations among subtests of IQ tests come about because all of these tasks in fact measure the ability to respond rapidly to items of a logical-mathematical or linguistic sort; we believe that these correlations would be substantially reduced if one were to survey in a contextually appropriate way the full range of human problem-solving skills.

Until now, we have supported the fiction that adult roles depend largely on the flowering of a single intelligence. In fact, however, nearly every cultural role of any degree of sophistication requires a combination of intelligences. Thus, even an apparently straightforward role, like playing the violin, transcends a reliance on simple musical intelligence. To become a successful violinist requires bodily-kinesthetic dexterity and the interpersonal skills of relating to an audience and, in a different way, choosing a manager; quite possibly it involves an intrapersonal intelligence as well. Dance requires skills in bodily-kinesthetic, musical, interpersonal, and spatial intelligences in varying degrees. Politics requires an interpersonal skill, a linguistic facility, and perhaps some logical aptitude. Inasmuch as nearly every cultural role requires several intelligences, it becomes important to consider individuals as a collection of aptitudes rather than as having a singular problem-solving faculty that can be measured directly through pencil-and-paper tests. Even given a relatively small number of such intelligences, the diversity of human ability is created through the differences in these profiles. In fact, it may well be that the "total is greater than the sum of the parts." An individual may not be particularly gifted in any intelligence; and yet, because of a particular combination or blend of skills, he or she may be able to fill some niche uniquely well. Thus it is of paramount importance to assess the particular combination of skills that may earmark an individual for a certain vocational or avocational niche.

Questions for Writing and Discussion

1. How does your view of intelligence compare with the traditional view that Gardner states in his first paragraph? How does it compare to Gardner's view? Of the three, which seems most reasonable? Why?

2. Gardner writes ". . .the biological proclivity to participate in a particular form of problem-solving must be coupled with cultural nurturing of that domain." Which of the seven intelligences seems to come most naturally to you? In what ways has this intelligence or "form of problem-solving" been nurtured? Write a paragraph (like the ones that Gardner uses to exemplify each type of intelligence) that shows you demonstrating your particular intellectual strength.

3. In Gardner's conclusion, he asserts that in order to be successful in a specific "cultural role" one must cultivate a combination of intelligences. Consider a professional field or cultural role that you aspire to. What intelligences will you need to be successful in this role? How will you continue developing these intelligences?

4. Of the intelligences that Gardner discusses, which is most challenging for you to acquire? Why? Are you motivated to work at developing this type of intelligence within yourself? Why or why not?

MAKING IT MATTER

When you get a writing assignment, do you ever panic about how to write the minimum number of words required, labor over "sounding intelligent," or simply ask yourself, "What does this professor want?"

BREAKING IT DOWN

Paul Roberts uses humor to dispense his advice to students. What effect does his use of humor have on you as a reader?

How to Say Nothing in 500 Words
PAUL ROBERTS

Paul Roberts (1917–1967) taught college English for over 20 years, first at San Jose State College and later at Cornell University. He was a scholar of linguistics and author of many textbooks. The following selection is taken from one of this best-known texts, Understanding English (1958).

◆

NOTHING ABOUT SOMETHING

It's Friday afternoon, and you have almost survived another week of classes. You are just looking forward dreamily to the weekend when the English instructor says: "For Monday you will turn in a five-hundred-word composition on college football."

Well, that puts a good big hole in the weekend. You don't have any strong views on college football one way or the other. You get rather excited during the season and go to all the home games and find it rather more fun than not. On the other hand, the class has been reading Robert Hutchins in the anthology and perhaps Shaw's "Eighty-Yard Run," and from the class discussion you have got the idea that the instructor thinks college football is for the birds. You are no fool, you. You can figure out what side to take.

After dinner you get out the portable typewriter that you got for high school graduation. You might as well get it over with and enjoy Saturday and Sunday. Five hundred words is about two double-spaced pages with normal margins. You put in a sheet of paper, think up a title, and you're off:

Why College Football Should Be Abolished

College football should be abolished because it's bad for the school and also bad for the players. The players are so busy practicing that they don't have any time for their studies.

This, you feel, is a mighty good start. The only trouble is that it's only thirty-two words. You still have four hundred and sixty-eight to go, and you've pretty well exhausted the subject. It comes to you that you do your best thinking in the morning, so you put away the typewriter and go to the movies. But the next morning you have to do your washing and some math problems, and in the afternoon you go to the game. The English instructor turns up too, and you wonder if you've taken the right side after all. Saturday night you have a date, and Sunday morning you have to go to church. (You shouldn't let English assignments interfere with your religion.) What with one thing and another, it's ten o'-clock Sunday night before you get out the typewriter again. You make a pot of coffee and start to fill out your views on college football. Put a little meat on the bones.

Why College Football Should Be Abolished

In my opinion, it seems to me that college football should be abolished. The reason why I think this to be true is because I feel that football is bad for the colleges in nearly every respect. As Robert Hutchins says in his article in our anthology in which he discusses college football, it would be better if the colleges had race horses and had races with one another, because then the horses would not have to attend classes. I firmly agree with Mr. Hutchins on this point, and I am sure that many other students would agree too.

One reason why it seems to me that college football is bad is that it has become too commercial. In the olden times when people played football just for the fun of it, maybe college football was all right, but they do not play football just for the fun of it now as they used to in the old days. Nowadays college football is what you might call a big business. Maybe this is not true at all schools, and I don't think it is especially true here at State, but certainly this is the case at most colleges and universities in America nowadays, as Mr. Hutchins points out in his very interesting article. Actually the coaches and alumni go around to the high schools and offer the high school stars large salaries to come to their colleges and play football for them. There was one case where a high school star was offered a convertible if he would play football for a certain college.

Another reason for abolishing college football is that it is bad for the players. They do not have time to get a college education, because they are so busy playing football. A football player has to practice every afternoon from three to six, and then he is so tired that he can't concentrate on his studies. He just feels like dropping off to sleep after dinner, and then the next day he goes to his classes without having studied and maybe he fails the test.

(Good ripe stuff so far, but you're still a hundred and fifty-one words from home. One more push.)

Also I think college football is bad for the colleges and the universities because not very many students get to participate in it. Out of a college of ten thousand students only seventy-five or a hundred play football, if that many. Football is what you might call a spectator sport. That means that most people go to watch it but do not play it themselves.

(Four hundred and fifteen. Well, you still have the conclusion, and when you retype it, you can make the margins a little wider.)

These are the reasons why I agree with Mr. Hutchins that college football should be abolished in American colleges and universities.

On Monday you turn it in, moderately hopeful, and on Friday it comes back marked "weak in content" and sporting a big "D."

This essay is exaggerated a little, not much. The English instructor will recognize it as reasonably typical of what an assignment on college football will bring in. He knows that nearly half of the class will contrive in five hundred words to say that college football is too commercial and bad for the players. Most of the other half will inform him that college football builds character and prepares one for life and brings prestige to the school. As he reads paper after paper all saying the same thing in almost the same words, all bloodless, five hundred words dripping out of nothing, he wonders how he allowed himself to get trapped into teaching English when he might have had a happy and interesting life as an electrician or a confidence man.

Well, you may ask, what can you do about it? The subject is one on which you have few convictions and little information. Can you be expected to make a dull subject interesting? As a matter of fact, this is precisely what you are expected to do. This is the writer's essential task. All subjects, except sex, are dull until somebody makes them interesting. The writer's job is to find the argument, the approach, the angle, the wording that will take the reader with him. This is seldom easy, and it is particularly hard in subjects that have been much discussed: College Football, Fraternities, Popular Music, Is Chivalry Dead?, and the like. You will feel that there is nothing you can do with such subjects except repeat the old bromides. But there are some things you can do which will make your papers, if not throbbingly alive, at least less insufferably tedious than they might otherwise be.

AVOID THE OBVIOUS CONTENT

Say the assignment is college football. Say that you've decided to be against it. Begin by putting down the arguments that come to your mind: it is too commercial, it takes the students' minds off their studies, it is hard on the players, it makes the university a kind of circus instead of an intellectual center, for most schools it is financially ruinous. Can you think of any more arguments just off hand? All right. Now when you write your paper, *make sure that you don't use any of the material on this list.* If these are the points that leap to your mind, they will leap to everyone else's too, and whether you get a "C" or a "D" may depend on whether the instructor reads your paper early when he is fresh and tolerant or late, when the sentence "In my opinion, college football has become too commercial," inexorably repeated, has brought him to the brink of lunacy.

Be against college football for some reason or reasons of your own. If they are keen and perceptive ones, that's splendid. But even if they are trivial or foolish or indefensible, you are still ahead so long as they are not everybody else's reasons too. Be against it because the colleges don't spend enough money on it to make it worth while, because it is bad for the characters of the spectators, because the players are forced to attend classes, because the football stars hog all the beautiful women, because it competes with baseball and is therefore un-American and possibly

Communist inspired. There are lots of more or less unused reasons for being against college football.

Sometimes it is a good idea to sum up and dispose of the trite and conventional points before going on to your own. This has the advantage of indicating to the reader that you are going to be neither trite nor conventional. Something like this:

> We are often told that college football should be abolished because it has become too commercial or because it is bad for the players. These arguments are no doubt very cogent, but they don't really go to the heart of the matter.

Then you go to the heart of the matter.

TAKE THE LESS USUAL SIDE

One rather simple way of getting interest into your paper is to take the side of the argument that most of the citizens will want to avoid. If the assignment is an essay on dogs, you can, if you choose, explain that dogs are faithful and lovable companions, intelligent, useful as guardians of the house and protectors of children, indispensable in police work—in short, when all is said and done, man's best friends. Or you can suggest that those big brown eyes conceal, more often than not, a vacuity of mind and an inconstancy of purpose; that the dogs you have known most intimately have been mangy, ill-tempered brutes, incapable of instruction; and that only your nobility of mind and fear of arrest prevent you from kicking the flea-ridden animals when you pass them on the street.

Naturally, personal convictions will sometimes dictate your approach. If the assigned subject is "Is Methodism Rewarding to the Individual?" and you are a pious Methodist, you have really no choice. But few assigned subjects, if any, will fall in this category. Most of them will lie in broad areas of discussion with much to be said on both sides. They are intellectual exercises and it is legitimate to argue now one way and now another, as debaters do in similar circumstances. Always take the side that looks to you hardest, least defensible. It will almost always turn out to be easier to write interestingly on that side.

This general advice applies where you have a choice of subjects. If you are to choose among "The Value of Fraternities" and "My Favorite High School Teacher" and "What I Think About Beetles," by all means plump for the beetles. By the time the instructor gets to your paper, he will be up to his ears in tedious tales about the French teacher at Bloombury High and assertions about how fraternities build character and prepare one for life. Your views on beetles, whatever they are, are bound to be a refreshing change.

Don't worry too much about figuring out what the instructor thinks about the subject so that you can cuddle up with him. Chances are his views are no stronger than yours. If he does have convictions and you oppose them, his problem is to keep from grading you higher than you deserve in order to show he is not biased. This doesn't mean that you should always cantankerously dissent from what the instructor says; that gets tiresome too. And if the subject assigned is "My Pet Peeve," do not begin, "My pet peeve is the English instructor who assigns papers on 'my pet peeve.'" This was still funny during the War of 1812, but it has sort of lost its edge since then. It is in general good manners to avoid personalities.

SLIP OUT OF ABSTRACTION

If you will study the essay on college football . . . you will perceive that one reason for its appalling dullness is that it never gets down to particulars. It is just a series of not very glittering generalities: "football is bad for the colleges," "it has become too commercial," "football is a big business," "it is bad for the players," and so on. Such round phrases thudding against the reader's brain are unlikely to convince him, though they may well render him unconscious.

If you want the reader to believe that college football is bad for the players, you have to do more than say so. You have to display the evil. Take your roommate, Alfred Simkins, the second-string center. Picture poor old Alfy coming home from football practice every evening, bruised and aching, agonizingly tired, scarcely able to shovel the mashed potatoes into his mouth. Let us see him staggering up to the room, getting out his econ textbook, peering desperately at it with his good eye, falling asleep and failing the test in the morning. Let us share his unbearable tension as Saturday draws near. Will he fail, be demoted, lose his monthly allowance, be forced to return to the coal mines? And if he succeeds, what will be his reward? Perhaps a slight ripple of applause when the third-string center replaces him, a moment of elation in the locker room if the team wins, of despair if it loses.

What will he look back on when he graduates from college? Toil and torn ligaments. And what will be his future? He is not good enough for pro football, and he is too obscure and weak in econ to succeed in stocks and bonds. College football is tearing the heart from Alfy Simkins and, when it finishes with him, will callously toss aside the shattered hulk.

This is no doubt a weak enough argument for the abolition of college football, but it is a sight better than saying, in three or four variations, that college football (in your opinion) is bad for the players.

Look at the work of any professional writer and notice how constantly he is moving from the generality, the abstract statement, to the concrete example, the facts and figures, the illustration. If he is writing on juvenile delinquency, he does not just tell you that juveniles are (it seems to him) delinquent and that (in his opinion) something should be done about it. He shows you juveniles being delinquent, tearing up movie theatres in Buffalo, stabbing high school principals in Dallas, smoking marijuana in Palo Alto. And more than likely he is moving toward some specific remedy, not just a general wringing of the hands.

It is no doubt possible to be *too* concrete, too illustrative or anecdotal, but few inexperienced writers err this way. For most the soundest advice is to be seeking always for the picture, to be always turning general remarks into seeable examples. Don't say, "Sororities teach girls the social graces." Say "Sorority life teaches a girl how to carry on a conversation while pouring tea, without sloshing the tea into the saucer." Don't say, "I like certain kinds of popular music very much." Say, "Whenever I hear Gerber Spinklittle play 'Mississippi Man' on the trombone, my socks creep up my ankles."

GET RID OF OBVIOUS PADDING

The student toiling away at his weekly English theme is too often tormented by a figure: five hundred words. How, he asks himself, is he to achieve this staggering total? Obviously by never using one word when he can somehow work in ten.

He is therefore seldom content with a plain statement like "Fast driving is dangerous." This has only four words in it. He takes thought, and the sentence becomes:

In my opinion, fast driving is dangerous.

Better, but he can do better still:

> In my opinion, fast driving would seem to be rather dangerous.

If he is really adept, it may come out:

> In my humble opinion, though I do not claim to be an expert on this complicated subject, fast driving, in most circumstances, would seem to be rather dangerous in many respects, or at least so it would seem to me.

Thus four words have been turned into forty, and not an iota of content has been added.

Now this is a way to go about reaching five hundred words, and if you are content with a "D" grade, it is as good a way as any. But if you aim higher, you must work differently. Instead of stuffing your sentences with straw, you must try steadily to get rid of the padding, to make your sentences lean and tough. If you are really working at it, your first draft will greatly exceed the required total, and then you will work it down, thus:

> It is thought in some quarters that fraternities do not contribute as much as might be expected to campus life.
> Some people think that fraternities contribute little to campus life.
> > The average doctor who practices in small towns or in the country must toil night and day to heal the sick.
> > Most country doctors work long hours.
> > When I was a little girl, I suffered from shyness and embarrassment in the presence of others.
> > I was a shy little girl.
> > It is absolutely necessary for the person employed as a marine fireman to give the matter of steam pressure his undivided attention at all times.
> > The fireman has to keep his eye on the steam gauge.

You may ask how you can arrive at five hundred words at this rate. Simply. You dig up more real content. Instead of taking a couple of obvious points off the surface of the topic and then circling warily around them for six paragraphs, you work in and explore, figure out the details. You illustrate. You say that fast driving is dangerous, and then you prove it. How long does it take to stop a car at forty and at eighty? How far can you see at night? What happens when a tire blows? What happens in a head-on collision at fifty miles an hour? Pretty soon your paper will be full of broken glass and blood and headless torsos, and reaching five hundred words will not really be a problem.

CALL A FOOL A FOOL

Some of the padding in freshman themes is to be blamed not on anxiety about the word minimum but on excessive timidity. The student writes, "In my opinion, the principal of my high school acted in ways that I believe every unbiased person would have to call foolish." This isn't exactly what he means. What he means is, "My high school principal was a fool." If he was a fool, call him a fool. Hedging the thing about with "in-my-opinion's" and "it-seems-to-me's" and "as-I-see-it's" and "at-least-from-my-point-of-view's" gains you nothing. Delete these phrases whenever they creep into your paper.

The student's tendency to hedge stems from a modesty that in other circumstances would be commendable. He is, he realizes, young and inexperienced, and he half suspects that he is dopey and fuzzy-minded beyond the average. Probably only too true. But it doesn't help to announce your incompetence six times in every paragraph. Decide what you want to say and say it as vigorously as possible, without apology and in plain words.

Linguistic diffidence can take various forms. One is what we call *euphemism*. This is the tendency to call a spade "a certain garden implement" or women's underwear "unmentionables." It is stronger in some eras than others and in some people than others but it always operates more or less in subjects that are touchy or taboo: death, sex, madness, and so on. Thus we shrink from saying "He died last night" but say instead "passed away," "left us," "joined his Maker," "went to his reward." Or we try to take off the tension with a lighter cliché: "kicked the bucket," "cashed in his chips," "handed in his dinner pail." We have found all sorts of ways to avoid saying *mad*: "mentally ill," "touched," "not quite right upstairs," "feeble-minded," "innocent," "simple," "off his trolley," "not in his right mind." Even such a now plain word as *insane* began as a euphemism with the meaning "not healthy."

Modern science, particularly psychology, contributes many polysyllables in which we can wrap our thoughts and blunt their force. To many writers there is no such thing as a bad schoolboy. Schoolboys are maladjusted or unoriented or misunderstood or in need of guidance or lacking in continued success toward satisfactory integration of the personality as a social unit, but they are never bad. Psychology no doubt makes us better men or women, more sympathetic and tolerant, but it doesn't make writing any easier. Had Shakespeare been confronted with psychology, "To be or not to be" might have come out, "To continue as a social unit or not to do so. That is the personality problem. Whether 'tis a better sign of integration at the conscious level to display a psychic tolerance toward the maladjustments and repressions induced by one's lack of orientation in one's environment or-" But Hamlet would never have finished the soliloquy.

Writing in the modern world, you cannot altogether avoid modern jargon. Nor, in an effort to get away from euphemism, should you salt your paper with four-letter words. But you can do much if you will mount guard against those roundabout phrases, those echoing polysyllables that tend to slip into your writing to rob it of its crispness and force.

BEWARE OF THE PAT EXPRESSION

Other things being equal, avoid phrases like "other things being equal." Those sentences that come to you whole, or in two or three doughy lumps, are sure to be bad sentences. They are no creation of yours but pieces of common thought floating in the community soup.

Pat expressions are hard, often impossible, to avoid, because they come too easily to be noticed and seem too necessary to be dispensed with. No writer avoids them altogether, but good writers avoid them more often than poor writers.

By "pat expressions" we mean such tags as "to all practical intents and purposes," "the pure and simple truth," "from where I sit," "the time of his life," "to the ends of the earth," "in the twinkling of an eye," "as sure as you're born," "over my dead body," "under cover of darkness," "took the easy way out," "when all is said and done," "told him time and time again," "parted the best of friends," "stand up and be counted," "gave him the best years of her life," "worked her fingers to the bone." Like other clichés, these expressions were once forceful. Now we should use them only when we can't possibly think of anything else.

Some pat expressions stand like a wall between the writer and thought. Such a one is "the American way of life." Many student writers feel that when they have said that something accords with the American way of life or does not they have exhausted the subject. Actually, they have stopped at the highest level of abstraction. The American way of life is the complicated set of bonds between a hundred and eighty million ways. All of us know this when we think about it, but the tag phrase too often keeps us from thinking about it.

So with many another phrase dear to the politician: "this great land of ours," "the man in the street," "our national heritage." These may prove our patriotism or give a clue to our political beliefs, but otherwise they add nothing to the paper except words.

COLORFUL WORDS

The writer builds with words, and no builder uses a raw material more slippery and elusive and treacherous. A writer's work is a constant struggle to get the right word in the right place, to find that particular word that will convey his meaning exactly, that will persuade the reader or soothe him or startle or amuse him. He never succeeds altogether—sometimes he feels that he scarcely succeeds at all—but such successes as he has are what make the thing worth doing.

There is no book of rules for this game. One progresses through everlasting experiment on the basis of ever-widening experience. There are few useful generalizations that one can make about words as words, but there are perhaps a few.

Some words are what we call "colorful." By this we mean that they are calculated to produce a picture or induce an emotion. They are dressy instead of plain, specific instead of general, loud instead of soft. Thus, in place of "Her heart beat," we may write "Her heart *pounded, throbbed, fluttered, danced.*" Instead of "He sat in his chair," we may say, "He *lounged, sprawled, coiled.*" Instead of "It was hot," we may say, "It was *blistering, sultry, muggy, suffocating, steamy, wilting.*"

However, it should not be supposed that the fancy word is always better. Often it is as well to write "Her heart beat" or "It was hot" if that is all it did or all it was. Ages differ in how they like their prose. The nineteenth century liked it rich and smoky. The twentieth has usually preferred it lean and cool. The twentieth-century writer, like all writers, is forever seeking the exact word, but he is wary of sounding feverish. He tends to pitch it low, to understate it, to throw it away. He knows that if he gets too colorful, the audience is likely to giggle.

See how this strikes you: "As the rich, golden glow of the sunset died away along the eternal western hills, Angela's limpid blue eyes looked softly and trustingly into Montague's flashing brown ones, and her heart pounded like a drum in time with the joyous song surging in her soul." Some people like that sort of thing, but most modern readers would say, "Good grief," and turn on the television.

COLORED WORDS

Some words we would call not so much colorful as colored—that is, loaded with associations, good or bad. All words—except perhaps structure words—have associations of some sort. We have said that the meaning of a word is the sum of the contexts in which it occurs. When we hear a word, we hear with it an echo of all the situations in which we have heard it before.

In some words, these echoes are obvious and discussable. The word *mother*, for example, has, for most people, agreeable associations. When you hear *mother* you probably think of home, safety, love, food, and various other pleasant things. If one writes, "She was like a mother to me," he gets an effect which he would not get in "She was like an aunt to me." The advertiser makes use of the associations of *mother* by working it in when he talks about his product. The politician works it in when he talks about himself.

So also with such words as *home, liberty, fireside, contentment, patriot, tenderness, sacrifice, childlike, manly, bluff, limpid*. All of these words are loaded with favorable associations that would be rather hard to indicate in a straightforward definition. There is more than a literal difference between "They sat around the fireside" and "They sat around the stove." They might have been equally warm and happy around the stove, but *fireside* suggests leisure, grace, quiet tradition, congenial company, and *stove* does not.

Conversely, some words have bad associations. *Mother* suggests pleasant things, but *mother-in-law* does not. Many mothers-in-law are heroically lovable and some mothers drink gin all day and beat their children insensible, but these facts of life are beside the point. The thing is that *mother* sounds good and *mother-in-law* does not.

Or consider the word *intellectual*. This would seem to be a complimentary term, but in point of fact it is not, for it has picked up associations of impracticality and ineffectuality and general dopiness. So also with such words as *liberal, reactionary, Communist, socialist, capitalist, radical, school-teacher, truck driver, undertaker, operator, salesman, huckster, speculator*. These convey meanings on the literal level, but beyond that—sometimes, in some places—they convey contempt on the part of the speaker.

The question of whether to use loaded words or not depends on what is being written. The scientist, the scholar, try to avoid them; for the poet, the advertising writer, the public speaker, they are standard equipment. But every writer should take care that they do not substitute for thought. If you write, "Anyone who thinks that is nothing but a Socialist (or Communist or capitalist)," you have said nothing except that you don't like people who think that, and such remarks are effective only with the most naïve readers. It is always a bad mistake to think your readers more naïve than they really are.

COLORLESS WORDS

But probably most student writers come to grief not with words that are colorful or those that are colored but with those that have no color at all. A pet example is *nice*, a word we would find it hard to dispense with in casual conversation but which is no longer capable of adding much to a description. Colorless words are those of such general meaning that in a particular sentence they mean nothing. Slang adjectives, like *cool* ("That's real cool") tend to explode all over the language. They are applied to everything, lose their original force, and quickly die.

Beware also of nouns of very general meaning, like *circumstances, cases, instances, aspects, factors, relationships, attitudes, eventualities*, etc. In most circumstances you will find that those cases of writing which contain too many instances of words like these will in this and other aspects have factors leading to unsatisfactory relationships with the reader resulting in unfavorable attitudes on his part and perhaps other eventualities, like a grade of "D." Notice also what "etc." means. It means "I'd like to make this list longer, but I can't think of any more examples."

Questions for Writing and Discussion

1. Can you relate to any of the issues that Roberts discusses in his piece? If so, which ones? How valuable do you think his advice is? If you find any of it (or all of it) valuable, how does he convince you that his advice is worthy of your consideration? If you don't find it valuable, what makes you reject his advice?

2. Roberts has a lot of experience as a writing professor and has, clearly, read many student essays. Write a process analysis or "how-to" essay about

something you know a lot about. Make sure it's addressed to a specific audience (teachers, college students, high school students, customers of a place where you work, or another group that you could advise based on your expertise). Use humor to convey your point, if applicable.

3. Roberts writes, "Some pat expressions stand like a wall between the writer and thought." He then goes on to explain that certain pat expressions are "dear to politicians." What do you think of Roberts' suggestion that politicians use pat expressions to appeal to our emotions? Go to the website of your favorite or least favorite politician and read some of his or her speeches. Analyze that politician's use of pat phrases or clichés and discuss the impact this has on you as a voter.

4. Roberts uses metaphors and similes to create images in the mind of the reader and to explain the nature of writing by comparing it to more familiar concepts. One is stated in Question 3 ("stand like a wall") and another is "The writer builds with words, and no builder uses a raw material more slippery and elusive and treacherous." Develop your own simile or metaphor for writing and explain how your comparison captures your experience with writing.

MAKING IT MATTER

Tracking is a system in which students are placed in high, low, or mid-level classes based on test scores or demonstrated ability in an earlier grade. Have you ever been part of a school system that uses tracking? If so, did this system serve you well? Do you think tracking, or ability-based grouping, is an effective educational technique? Why or why not?

BREAKING IT DOWN

As you read this selection, notice the diction that Rose uses. Whom do you think his primary audience is?

I Just Wanna Be Average
MIKE ROSE

Mike Rose is a professor at the University of California at Los Angeles Graduate School of Education and Information Studies and a nationally recognized expert on class, ethnicity, and culture in the American educational system. The following selection is taken from his book Lives on the Boundary *(1989).*

───────────── ✦ ─────────────

It took two buses to get to Our Lady of Mercy. The first started deep in South Los Angeles and caught me at midpoint. The second drifted through neighborhoods with trees, parks, big lawns, and lots of flowers. The rides were long but were livened up by a group of South LA veterans whose parents also thought that Hope had set up shop in the west end of the county. There was Christy Biggars, who, at sixteen, was dealing and was, according to rumor, a pimp as well. There were Bill Cobb and Johnny Gonzales, grease-pencil artists extraordinaire, who left Nembutal-enhanced swirls of "Cobb" and "Johnny" on the corrugated walls of the bus. And then there was Tyrrell Wilson. Tyrrell was the coolest kid I knew. He ran the dozens like a metric halfback, laid down a rap that outrhymed and outpointed Cobb, whose rap was good but not great—the curse of a moderately soulful kid trapped in white skin. But it was Cobb who would sneak a radio onto the bus, and thus underwrote his patter with Little Richard, Fats Domino, Chuck Berry, the Coasters, and Ernie K. Doe's mother-in-law, an awful woman who was "sent from down below." And so it was that Christy and Cobb and Johnny G. and Tyrrell and assorted others picked up along the way passed our days in the back of the bus, a funny mix brought together by geography and parental desire.

Entrance to school brings with it forms and releases and assessments. Mercy relied on a series of tests, mostly the Stanford-Binet, for placement, and somehow the results of my tests got confused with those of another student named Rose. The other Rose apparently didn't do very well, for I was placed in the vocational track, a euphemism for the bottom level. Neither I nor my parents realized what this meant We had no sense that Business Math, Typing, and English-Level D were dead ends. The current state of reports on the schools criticizes parents for not involving themselves in the education of their children. But how would someone like Tommy Rose, with his two years of Italian schooling, know what to ask? And what sort of pressure could an exhausted waitress apply? The error went undetected, and I remained in the vocational track for two years. What a place.

My homeroom was supervised by Brother Dill, a troubled and unstable man who also taught freshman English. When his class drifted away from him, which was often, his voice would rise in paranoid accusations, and occasionally he would lose control and shake or smack us. I hadn't been there two months when one of his brisk, face-turning slaps had my glasses sliding down the aisle. Physical education was also pretty harsh. Our teacher was a stubby ex-lineman who had played old-time pro ball in the Midwest. He routinely had us grabbing our ankles to receive his stinging paddle across our butts. He did that, he said, to make men of us. "Rose," he bellowed on our first encounter; me standing geeky in line in my baggy shorts. "Rose"? What the hell kind of name is that?"

"Italian, sir," I squeaked.

"Italian! Ho. Rose, do you know the sound a bag of shit makes when it hits the wall?"

"No, sir."

"Wop!"

Sophomore English was taught by Mr. Mitropetros. He was a large, bejeweled man who managed the parking lot at the Shrine Auditorium. He would crow and preen and list for us the stars he'd brushed against. We'd ask questions and glance knowingly and snicker, and all that fueled the poor guy to brag some more. Parking cars was his night job. He had little training in English, so his lesson plan for his day work had us reading the district's required text, *Julius Caesar*, aloud for the semester. We'd finish the play way before the twenty weeks was up, so he'd have us switch parts again and again and start again: Dave Snyder, the fastest guy at Mercy, muscling through Caesar to the breathless squeals of Calpurnia, as interpreted by Steve Fusco, a surfer who owned the school's most envied paneled wagon. Week ten and Dave and Steve would take on new roles, as would we all, and render a water-logged Cassius and a Brutus that are beyond my powers of description.

Spanish I—taken in the second year—fell into the hands of a new recruit. Mr. Montez was a tiny man, slight, five foot six at the most, soft-spoken and delicate. Spanish was a particularly rowdy class, and Mr. Montez was as prepared for it as a doily maker at a hammer throw. He would tap his pencil to a room in which Steven Fusco was propelling spitballs from his heavy lips, in which Mike Dweetz was taunting Bill Hawk, a half-Indian, half-Spanish,

reed-thin, quietly explosive boy. The vocational track at Our Lady
of Mercy mixed kids traveling in from South L.A. with South Bay
surfers and a few Slavs and Chicanos from the harbors of San
Pedro. This was a dangerous miscellany: surfers and hodads and
South-Central blacks all ablaze to the metronomic tapping of
Hector Montez's pencil.

One day Billy lost it. Out of the comer of my eye I saw him
strike out with his right arm and catch Dweetz across the neck.
Quick as a spasm, Dweetz was out of his seat, scattering desks,
cracking Billy on the side of the head, right behind the eye.
Snyder and Fusco and others broke it up, but the room felt hot
and close and naked. Mr. Montez's tenuous authority was finally
ripped to shreds, and I think everyone felt a little strange about
that. The charade was over, and when it came down to it, I don't
think any of the kids really wanted it to end this way. They had
pushed and pushed and bullied their way into a freedom that
both scared and embarrassed them.

Students will float to the mark you set. I and the others in the
vocational classes were bobbing in pretty shallow water.
Vocational education has aimed at increasing the economic opportunities of students who do not do well in our schools. Some
serious programs succeed in doing that and through exceptional
teachers—like Mr. Gross in *Horace's Compromise*—students learn
to develop hypotheses and troubleshoot, reason through a problem, and communicate effectively—the true job skills. The vocational track, however, is most often a place for those who are just
not making it, a dumping ground for the disaffected. There were a
few teachers who worked hard at education; young Brother
Slattery, for example, combined a stern voice with weekly quizzes
to try to pass along to us a skeletal outline of world history. But
mostly the teachers had no idea of how to engage the imaginations
of us kids who were scuttling along at the bottom of the pond.

And the teachers would have needed some inventiveness, for
none of us was groomed for the classroom. It wasn't just that I
didn't know things—didn't know how to simplify algebraic fractions, couldn't identify different kinds of clauses, bungled Spanish
translations—but that I had developed various faulty and inade-
quate ways of doing algebra and making sense of Spanish. Worse
yet, the years of defensive tuning out in elementary school had
given me a way to escape quickly while seeming at least half alert.
During my time in Voc Ed., I developed further into a mediocre

student and a somnambulant problem solver, and that affected the subjects I did have the wherewithal to handle: I detested Shakespeare; I got bored with history. My attention flitted here and there. I fooled around in class and read my books indifferently—the intellectual equivalent of playing with your food. I did what I had to do to get by, and I did it with half a mind.

But I did learn things about people and eventually came into my own socially. I liked the guys in Voc. Ed. Growing up where I did, I understood and admired physical prowess, and there was an abundance of muscle here. There was Dave Snyder, a sprinter and halfback of true quality. Dave's ability and his quick wit gave him a natural appeal, and he was welcome in any clique, though he always kept a little independent. He enjoyed acting the fool and could care less about studies, but he possessed a certain maturity and never caused the faculty much trouble. It was a testament to his independence that he included me among his friends—I eventually went out for track, but I was no jock. Owing to the Latin alphabet and a dearth of *Rs* and *Ss*, Snyder sat behind Rose, and we started exchanging one-liners and became friends.

There was Ted Richard, a much-touted Little League pitcher. He was chunky and had a baby face and came to Our Lady of Mercy as a seasoned street fighter. Ted was quick to laugh and he had a loud, jolly laugh; but when he got angry he'd smile a little smile, the kind that simply raises the corner of the mouth a quarter of an inch. For those who knew, it was an eerie signal. Those who didn't found themselves in big trouble, for Ted was very quick. He loved to carry on what we would come to call philosophical discussions: What is courage? Does God exist? He also loved words, enjoyed picking up big ones like *salubrious* and *equivocal* and using them in our conversations—laughing at himself as the word hit a chuckhole rolling off his tongue. Ted didn't do all that well in school—baseball and parties and testing the courage he'd speculated about took up his time. His textbooks were *Argosy* and *Field and Stream,* whatever newspapers he'd find on the bus stop—from the *Daily Worker* to pornography—conversations with uncles and hobos or businessmen he'd meet in a coffee shop. *The Old Man and the Sea.* With hindsight, I can see that Ted was developing into one of those rough-hewn intellectuals whose sources are a mix of the learned and the apocryphal, whose discussions are both assured and sad.

And then there was Ken Harvey. Ken was good-looking in a puffy way and had a full and oily ducktail and was a car enthusiast . . . a hodad. One day in religion class, he said the sentence that turned out to be one of the most memorable of the hundreds of thousands I heard in those Voc. Ed. years. We were talking about the parable of the talents, about achievement, working hard, doing the best you can do, blah-blah-blah, when the teacher called on the restive Ken Harvey for an opinion. Ken thought about it, but just for a second, and said (with studied, minimal affect), "I just wanna be average." That woke me up. Average?! Who wants to be average? Then the athletes chimed in with the clichés that make you want to laryngectomize them, and the exchange became a platitudinous melee. At the time, I thought Ken's assertion was stupid, and I wrote him off. But his sentence has stayed with me all these years, and I think I am finally coming to understand it.

Ken Harvey was gasping for air. School can be a tremendously disorienting place. No matter how bad the school, you're going to encounter notions that don't fit with the assumptions and beliefs that you grew up with—maybe you'll hear these dissonant notions from teachers, maybe from the other students, and maybe you'll read them. You'll also be thrown in with all kinds of kids from all lands and backgrounds, and that can be unsettling—this is especially true in places of rich ethnic and linguistic mix, like the L.A. basin. You'll see a handful of students far excel you in courses that sound exotic and that are only in the curriculum of the elite. French, physics, trigonometry. And all this is happening while you're trying to shape an identity, your body is changing, and your emotions are running wild. If you're a working-class kid in the vocational track, the options you'll have to deal with this will be constrained in certain ways: You're defined by your school as "slow"; you're placed in a curriculum that isn't designed to liberate you but to occupy you, or, if you're lucky, train you, though the training is for work the society does not esteem; other students are picking up the cues from your school and your curriculum and interacting with you in particular ways. If you're a kid like Ted Richard, you turn your back on all this and let your mind roam where it may. But youngsters like Ted are rare. What Ken and so many others do is protect themselves from such suffocating madness by taking on with a vengeance the identity implied in the vocational track. Reject the confusion and frustration by openly defining yourself as the Common Joe. Champion the average. Rely on your own good sense. Fuck this bullshit. Bullshit, of course, is everything you—and the others—fear is beyond you: books, essays, tests, academic scrambling, complexity, scientific reasoning, philosophical inquiry.

The tragedy is that you have to twist the knife in your own gray matter to make this defense work. You'll have to shut down, have to reject intellectual stimuli or diffuse them with sarcasm, have to cultivate stupidity, have to convert boredom from a malady into a way of confronting the world. Keep your vocabulary simple, act stoned when you're not or act more stoned than you are, flaunt ignorance, materialize your dreams. It is a powerful and effective defense—it neutralizes the insult and the frustration of being a vocational kid and, when perfected, it drives teachers up the wall, a delightful secondary effect. But like all strong magic, it exacts a price.

My own deliverance from the Voc. Ed. world began with sophomore biology. Every student, college prep to vocational, had to take biology, and unlike the other courses, the same person taught all sections. When teaching the vocational group, Brother Clint probably slowed down a bit or omitted a little of the fundamental biochemistry, but he used the same book and more or less the same syllabus across the board. If one class got tough, he could get tougher. He was young and powerful and very handsome, and looks and physical strength were high currency. No one gave him any trouble.

I was pretty bad at the dissecting table, but the lectures and the textbook were interesting: plastic overlays that, with each turned page, peeled away skin, then veins and muscle, then organs, down to the very bones that Brother Clint, pointer in hand, would tap out on our hanging skeleton. Dave Snyder was in big trouble, for the study of life—versus the living of it—was sticking in his craw. We worked out a code for our multiple-choice exams. He'd poke me in the back: once for the answer under A, twice for B, and so on; and when he'd hit the right one, I'd look up to the ceiling as though I were lost in thought. Poke: cytoplasm. Poke, poke: methane. Poke, poke, poke: William Harvey. Poke, poke, poke, poke: islets of Langerhans. This didn't work out perfectly, but Dave passed the course, and I mastered the dreamy look of a guy on a record jacket. And something else happened. Brother Clint puzzled over this Voc. Ed. kid who was racking up 98s and 99s on his tests. He checked the school's records and discovered the error. He recommended that I begin my junior year in the College Prep program. According to all I've read since, such a shift, as one report put it, is virtually impossible. Kids at that level rarely cross tracks. The telling thing is how chancy both my placement into and exit from Voc. Ed. was; neither I nor my parents had anything to do with it. I lived in one world during spring semester, and when I came back to school in the fall, I was living in another.

Switching to College Prep was a mixed blessing. I was an erratic student. I was undisciplined. And I hadn't caught onto the rules of the game: Why work hard in a class that didn't grab my fancy? I was also hopelessly behind in math. Chemistry was hard; toying with my chemistry set years before hadn't prepared me for the chemist's equations. Fortunately, the priest who taught both chemistry and second-year algebra was also the school's athletic director. Membership on the track team covered me; I knew I wouldn't get lower than a C. United States history was taught pretty well, and I did okay. But civics was taken over by a football coach who had trouble reading the textbook aloud—and reading aloud was the centerpiece of his pedagogy. College Prep at Mercy was certainly an improvement over the vocational program—at least it carried some status—but the social science curriculum was weak, and the mathematics and physical sciences were simply beyond me. I had a miserable quantitative background and ended up copying some assignments and finessing the rest as best I could. Let me try to explain how it feels to see again and again material you should once have learned but didn't.

You are given a problem. It requires you to simplify algebraic fractions or to multiply expressions containing square roots. You know this is pretty basic material because you've seen it for years. Once a teacher took some time with you, and you learned how to carry out these operations. Simple versions, anyway. But that was a year or two or more in the past, and these are more complex versions, and now you're not sure. And this, you keep telling yourself, is ninth- or even eighth-grade stuff.

Next it's a word problem. This is also old hat. The basic elements are as familiar as story characters: trains speeding so many miles per hour or shadows of buildings angling so many degrees. Maybe you know enough, have sat through enough explanations, to be able to begin setting up the problem: "If one train is going this fast . . ." or "This shadow is really one line of a triangle. . . ."

Then: "Let's see . . ." "How did Jones do this?" "Hmmmm." "No." "No, that won't work." Your attention wavers. You wonder about other things: a football game, a dance, that cute new checker at the market. You try to focus on the problem again. You scribble on paper for a while, but the tension wins out and your attention flits elsewhere. You crumple the paper and begin daydreaming to ease the frustration.

The particulars will vary, but in essence that is what a number of students go through, especially those in so-called remedial classes. They open their textbooks and see once again the familiar and impenetrable formulas and diagrams and terms that have stumped them for years. There is no excitement here. No excitement. Regardless of what the teacher says, this is not a new challenge. There is, rather, embarrassment and frustration and, not surprisingly, some anger in being reminded once again of long-standing inadequacies. No wonder so many students finally attribute their difficulties to something inborn, organic: "That part of my brain just doesn't work." Given the troubling histories many of these students have, it's miraculous that any of them can lift the shroud of hopelessness sufficiently to make deliverance from these classes possible.

Through this entire period, my father's health was deteriorating with cruel momentum. His arteriosclerosis progressed to the point where a simple nick on his shin wouldn't heal. Eventually it ulcerated and widened. Lou Minto would come by daily to change the dressing. We tried renting an oscillating bed—which we placed in the front room—to force blood through the constricted arteries in my father's legs. The bed hummed through the night, moving in place to ward off the inevitable. The ulcer continued to spread, and the doctors finally had to amputate. My grandfather had lost his leg in a stockyard accident. Now my father too was crippled. His convalescence was slow but steady, and the doctors placed him in the Santa Monica Rehabilitation Center, a sun-bleached building that opened out onto the warm spray of the Pacific. The place gave him some strength and some color and some training in walking with an artificial leg. He did pretty well for a year or so until he slipped and broke his hip. He was confined to a wheelchair after that, and the confinement contributed to the diminishing of his body and spirit.

I am holding a picture of him. He is sitting in his wheelchair and smiling at the camera. The smile appears forced, unsteady, seems to quaver, though it is frozen in silver nitrate. He is in his mid-sixties and looks eighty. Late in my junior year, he had a stroke and never came out of the resulting coma. After that, I would see him only in dreams, and to this day that is how I join him. Sometimes the dreams are sad and grisly and primal: my father lying in a bed soaked with his suppuration, holding me, rocking me. But sometimes the dreams bring him back to me healthy: him talking to me on an empty street, or buying some pictures to decorate our old house, or transformed somehow into someone strong and adept with tools and the physical.

Jack MacFarland couldn't have come into my life at a better time. My father was dead, and I had logged up too many years of scholastic indifference. Mr. MacFarland had a master's degree from Columbia and decided, at twenty-six, to find a little school and teach his heart out. He never took any credentialing courses, couldn't bear to, he said, so he had to find employment in a private system. He ended up at Our Lady of Mercy teaching five sections of senior English. He was a beatnik who was born too late. His teeth were stained, he tucked his sorry tie in between the third and fourth buttons of his shirt, and his pants were chronically wrinkled. At first, we couldn't believe this guy, thought he slept in his car. But within no time, he had us so startled with work that we didn't much worry about where he slept or if he slept at all. We wrote three or four essays a month. We read a book every two to three weeks, starting with the *Iliad* and ending up with Hemingway. He gave us a quiz on the reading every other day. He brought a prep school curriculum to Mercy High.

MacFarland's lectures were crafted, and as he delivered them he would pace the room jiggling a piece of chalk in his cupped hand, using it to scribble on the board the names of all the writers and philosophers and plays and novels he was weaving into his discussion. He asked questions often, raised everything from Zeno's paradox to the repeated last line of Frost's "Stopping by Woods on a Snowy Evening." He slowly and carefully built up our knowledge of Western intellectual history—with facts, with connections, with speculations. We learned about Greek philosophy, about Dante, the Elizabethan world view, the Age of Reason, existentialism. He analyzed poems with us, had us reading sections from John Ciardi's *How Does a Poem Mean?*, making a potentially difficult book accessible with his own explanations. We gave oral reports on poems Ciardi didn't cover. We imitated the styles of

Conrad, Hemingway, and *Time* magazine. We wrote and talked, wrote and talked. The man immersed us in language.

Even MacFarland's barbs were literary. If Jim Fitzsimmons, hung over and irritable, tried to smart-ass him, he'd rejoin with a flourish that would spark the indomitable Skip Madisor—who'd lost his front teeth in a hapless tackle—to flick his tongue through the gap and opine, "good chop," drawing out the single "o" in stinging indictment. Jack MacFarland, this tobacco-stained intellectual, brandished linguistic weapons of a kind I hadn't encountered before. He was this *egghead*, for God's sake, keeping some pretty difficult people in line. And from what I heard, Mike Dweetz and Steve Fusco and all the notorious Voc. Ed. crowd settled down as well when MacFarland took the podium. Though a lot of guys groused in the schoolyard, it just seemed that giving trouble to this particular teacher was a silly thing to do. Tomfoolery, not to mention assault, had no place in the world he was trying to create for us, and instinctively everyone knew that. If nothing else, we all recognized MacFarland's considerable intelligence and respected the hours he put into his work. It came to this: The troublemaker would look foolish rather than daring. Even Jim Fitzsimmons was reading *On the Road* and turning his incipient alcoholism to literary ends.

There were some lives that were already beyond Jack MacFarland's ministrations, but mine was not. I started reading again as I hadn't since elementary school. I would go into our gloomy little bedroom or sit at the dinner table while, on the television, Danny McShane was paralyzing Mr. Moto with the atomic drop, and work slowly back through *Heart of Darkness*, trying to catch the words in Conrad's sentences. I certainly was not MacFarland's best student; most of the other guys in College Prep, even my fellow slackers, had better backgrounds than I did. But I worked very hard, for MacFarland had hooked me. He tapped my old interest in reading and creating stories. He gave me a way to feel special by using my mind. And he provided a role model that wasn't shaped on physical prowess alone, and something inside me that I wasn't quite aware of responded to that. Jack MacFarland established a literacy club, to borrow a phrase of Frank Smith's, and invited me—invited all of us—to join.

There's been a good deal of research and speculation suggesting that the acknowledgment of school performance with extrinsic rewards—smiling faces, stars, numbers, grades—diminishes

the intrinsic satisfaction children experience by engaging in reading or writing or problem solving. While it's certainly true that
we've created an educational system that encourages our best and
brightest to become cynical grade collectors and, in general, have
developed an obsession with evaluation and assessment, I must
tell you that venal though it may have been, I loved getting good
grades from MacFarland. I now know how subjective grades can
be, but then they came tucked in the back of essays like bits of
scientific data, some sort of spectroscopic readout that said, objectively and publicly, that I had made something of value. I suppose I'd been mediocre for too long and enjoyed a public redefin-
ition. And I suppose the workings of my mind, such as they were,
had been private for too long. My linguistic play moved into the
world; like the intergalactic stories I told years before on Frank's
berry-splattered truck bed, these papers with their circled, red B-
pluses and A-minuses linked my mind to something outside it. I
carried them around like a club emblem.

One day in the December of my senior year, Mr. MacFarland
asked me where I was going to go to college. I hadn't thought
much about it. Many of the students I teach today spent their last
year in high school with a physics text in one hand and the
Stanford catalog in the other, but I wasn't even aware of what "entrance requirements" were. My folks would say that they wanted
me to go to college and be a doctor, but I don't know how seriously I ever took that; it seemed a sweet thing to say, a bit of sup-
portive family chatter, like telling a gangly daughter she's grace-
ful. The reality of higher education wasn't in my scheme of things.
No one in the family had gone to college; only two of my uncles
had completed high school. I figured I'd get a night job and go to
the local junior college because I knew that Snyder and Company
were going there to play ball. But I hadn't even prepared for that.
When I finally said, "I don't know," MacFarland looked down at
me—I was seated in his office—and said, "Listen, you can write."

My grades stank. I had A's in biology and a handful of B's in a
few English and social science classes. All the rest were C's—or
worse. MacFarland said I would do well in his class and laid
down the law about doing well in the others. Still, the record for
my first three years wouldn't have been acceptable to any four-
year school. To nobody's surprise, I was turned down flat by USC
and UCLA. But Jack MacFarland was on the case. He had received his bachelor's degree from Loyola University, so he made

calls to old professors and talked to somebody in admissions and wrote me a strong letter. Loyola finally accepted me as a probationary student. I would be on trial for the first year, and if I did okay, I would be granted regular status. MacFarland also intervened to get me a loan, for I could never have afforded a private college without it. Four more years of religion classes and four more years of boys at one school, girls at another. But at least I was going to college. Amazing.

In my last semester of high school, I elected a special English course fashioned by Mr. MacFarland, and it was through this elective that there arose at Mercy a fledgling literati. Art Mitz, the editor of the school newspaper and a very smart guy, was the kingpin. He was joined by me and by Mark Dever, a quiet boy who wrote beautifully and who would die before he was forty. MacFarland occasionally invited us to his apartment, and those visits became the high point of our apprenticeship: We'd clamp on our training wheels and drive to his salon.

He lived in a cramped and cluttered place near the airport, tucked away in the kind of building that architectural critic Reyner Baham calls a *dingbat*. Books were all over: stacked, piled, tossed, and crated, underlined and dog eared, well worn and new. Cigarette ashes crusted with coffee in saucers or spilled over the sides of motel ashtrays. The little bedroom had, along two of its walls, bricks and boards loaded with notes, magazines, and oversized books. The kitchen joined the living room, and there was a stack of German newspapers under the sink. I had never seen anything like it: a great flophouse of language furnished by City Lights and Cafe le Metro. I read every title. I flipped through paperbacks and scanned jackets and memorized names: Gogol, *Finnegan's Wake*, Djuna Barnes, Jackson Pollock, *A Coney Island of the Mind*, F. O. Matthiessen's *American Renaissance*, all sorts of Freud, *Troubled Sleep*, Man Ray, *The Education of Henry Adams*, Richard Wright, *Film as Art*, William Butler Yeats, Marguerite Duras, *Redburn*, *A Season in Hell*, *Kapital*. On the cover of Alain-Fournier's *The Wanderer* was an Edward Gorey drawing of a young man on a road winding into dark trees. By the hotplate sat a strange Kafka novel called *Amerika*, in which an adolescent hero crosses the Atlantic to find the Nature Theater of Oklahoma. Art and Mark would be talking about a movie or the school newspaper, and I would be consuming my English teacher's library. It was heady stuff. I felt like a Pop Warner athlete on steroids.

Art, Mark, and I would buy stogies and triangulate from MacFarland's apartment to the Cinema, which now shows X-rated films but was then L.A.'s premier art theater, and then to the musty Cherokee Bookstore in Hollywood to hobnob with beatnik homosexuals—smoking, drinking bourbon and coffee, and trying out awkward phrases we'd gleaned from our mentor's bookshelves. I was happy and precocious and a little scared as well, for Hollywood Boulevard was thick with a kind of decadence that was foreign to the South Side. After the Cherokee, we would head back to the security of MacFarland's apartment, slaphappy with hipness.

Let me be the first to admit that there was a good deal of adolescent passion in this embrace of the avant-garde: self-absorption, sexually charged pedantry, an elevation of the odd and abandoned. Still it was a time during which I absorbed an awful lot of information: long lists of titles, images from expressionist paintings, new wave shibboleths, snippets of philosophy, and names that read like Steve Fusco's misspellings—Goethe, Nietzsche, Kierkegaard. Now this is hardly the stuff of deep understanding. But it was an introduction, a phrase book, a Baedeker to a vocabulary of ideas, and it felt good at the time to know all these words. With hindsight I realize how layered and important that knowledge was.

It enabled me to do things in the world. I could browse bohemian book stores in far-off, mysterious Hollywood; I could go to the Cinema and see events through the lenses of European directors; and, most of all, I could share an evening, talk that talk, with Jack MacFarland, the man I most admired at the time. Knowledge was becoming a bonding agent. Within a year or two, the persona of the disaffected hipster would prove too cynical, too alienated to last. But for a time it was new and exciting: It provided a critical perspective on society, and it allowed me to act as though I were living beyond the limiting boundaries of South Vermont.

Questions for Writing and Discussion

1. Consider Rose's statement that "Students will float to the mark you set." Do you agree or disagree with this statement? Use examples from your own experience to support your position.

2. Make a list of the ten words from this essay that are most unfamiliar to you. Based on how the words are used, take a guess at what the words might mean. Then look them up and compare your "educated guesses" with the actual meanings. What effect did the use of these terms have on your interest in the piece?

3. Why did Rose carry around the grades he earned from Jack MacFarland "like a club emblem"? To what degree does your relationship or attitude about a particular teacher affect your performance in that teacher's class? Support your response with examples from your experience.

4. Rose suggests that "being a working class kid on the vocational track" can lead to a certain defensiveness. Summarize Rose's description of "the defense." Have you ever witnessed anyone using "the defense" as a way to cope? Describe the situation and what you think led this person to "shut down" in this way.

MAKING IT MATTER

Azar Nafisi writes about a small group of women she taught at her home because the Iranian government would not allow them to study certain works of literature in a public university. Consider the degree to which you value free speech and a free exchange of ideas. Is there anything that you are so passionate about learning that you would take personal risks to study it?

BREAKING IT DOWN

Consider Nafisi's choice to use flashback in her narrative. How does the use of flashback help to develop and clarify her thesis?

Upsilamba!
AZAR NAFISI

Azar Nafisi is a professor at Johns Hopkins University. Previously, she taught at the University of Tehran. She has written for the New York Times *and the* Washington Post, *among other nationally known publications. This selection is taken from her most recent book,* Reading Lolita in Tehran.

---◆---

U psilamba!" I heard Yassi exclaim as I entered the dining room with a tray of tea. Yassi loved playing with words. Once she told us that her obsession with words was pathological. As soon as I discover a new word, I have to use it, she said, like someone who buys an evening gown and is so eager that she wears it to the movies, or to lunch.

Let me pause and rewind the reel to retrace the events leading us to Yassi's exclamation. This was our first session. All of us had been nervous and inarticulate. We were used to meeting in public, mainly in classrooms and in lecture halls. The girls had their separate relationships with me, but except for Nassrin and Mahshid, who were intimate, and a certain friendship between Mitra and Sanaz, the rest were not close; in many cases, in fact, they would never have chosen to be friends. The collective intimacy made them uncomfortable.

I had explained to them the purpose of the class: to read, discuss and respond to works of fiction. Each would have a private diary, in which she should record her responses to the novels, as well as ways in which these works and their discussions related to her personal and social experiences. I explained that I had chosen them for this class because they seemed dedicated to the study of literature. I mentioned that one of the criteria for the books I had chosen was their authors' faith in the critical and almost magical power of literature, and reminded them of the nineteen-year-old Nabokov, who, during the Russian Revolution, would not allow himself to be diverted by the sound of bullets. He kept on writing his solitary poems while he heard the guns and saw the bloody fights from his window. Let us see, I said, whether seventy years later our disinterested faith will reward us by transforming the gloomy reality created of this other revolution.

The first work we discussed was *A Thousand and One Nights,* the familiar tale of the cuckolded king who slew successive virgin wives as revenge for his queen's betrayal, and whose murderous hand was finally stayed by the entrancing storyteller Scheherazade. I formulated certain general questions for them to consider, the most central of which was how these great works of imagination could help us in our present trapped situation as women. We were not looking for blueprints, for an easy solution, but we did hope to find a link between the open spaces the novels provided and the closed ones we were confined to. I remember reading to my girls Nabokov's claim that "readers were born free and ought to remain free."

What had most intrigued me about the frame story of *A Thousand and One Nights* were the three kinds of women it portrayed—all victims of a king's unreasonable rule. Before Scheherazade enters the scene, the women in the story are divided into those who betray and then are killed (the queen) and those who are killed before they have a chance to betray (the virgins). The virgins, who, unlike Scheherazade, have no voice in the story, are mostly ignored by the critics. Their silence, however, is significant. They surrender their virginity, and their lives, without resistance or protest. They do not quite exist, because they leave no trace in their anonymous death. The queen's infidelity does not rob the king of his absolute authority; it throws him off balance. Both types of women—the queen and the virgins—tacitly accept the king's public authority by acting within the confines of his domain and by accepting its arbitrary laws.

Scheherazade breaks the cycle of violence by choosing to embrace different terms of engagement. She fashions her universe not through physical force, as does the king, but through imagination and reflection. This gives her the courage to risk her life and sets her apart from the other characters in the tale.

Our edition of *A Thousand and One Nights* came in six volumes. I, luckily, had bought mine before it was banned and sold only on the black market, for exorbitant prices. I divided the volumes among the girls and asked them, for the next session, to classify the tales according to the types of women who played central roles in the stories.

Once I'd given them their assignment, I asked them each to tell the rest of us why they had chosen to spend their Thursday mornings here, discussing Nabokov and Jane Austen. Their answers were brief and forced. In order to break the ice, I suggested the calming distraction of cream puffs and tea.

This brings us to the moment when I enter the dining room with eight glasses of tea on an old and unpolished silver tray. Brewing and serving tea is an aesthetic ritual in Iran, performed several times a day. We serve tea in transparent glasses, small and shapely, the most popular of which is called slim-waisted: round and full at the top, narrow in the middle and round and full at the bottom. The color of the tea and its subtle aroma are an indication of the brewer's skill.

I step into the dining room with eight slim-waisted glasses whose honey-colored liquid trembles seductively. At this point, I hear Yassi shout triumphantly, "Upsilamba!" She throws the word at me like a ball, and I take a mental leap to catch it.

Upsilamba!—the word carries me back to the spring of 1994, when four of my girls and Nima were auditing a class I was teaching on the twentieth-century novel. The class's favorite book was Nabokov's *Invitation to a Beheading*. In this novel, Nabokov differentiates Cincinnatus C, his imaginative and lonely hero, from those around him through his originality in a society where uniformity is not only the norm but also the law. Even as a child, Nabokov tells us, Cincinnatus appreciated the freshness and beauty of language, while other children "understood each other at the first word, since they had no words that would end in an unexpected way, perhaps in some archaic letter, an upsilamba, becoming a bird or catapult with wondrous consequences."

No one in class had bothered to ask what the word meant. No one, that is, who was properly taking the class—for many of my old students just stayed on and sat in on my classes long after their graduation. Often, they were more interested and worked harder than my regular students, who were taking the class for credit. Thus it was that those who audited the class—including Nassrin, Manna, Nima, Mahshid and Yassi—had one day gathered in my office to discuss this and a number of other questions.

I decided to play a little game with the class, to test their curiosity. On the midterm exam, one of the questions was "Explain the significance of the word *upsilamba* in the context of *Invitation to a Beheading*. What does the word mean, and how does it relate to the main theme of the novel?" Except for four or five students, no one had any idea what I could possibly mean, a point I did not forget to remind them of every once in a while throughout the rest of that term.

The truth was that *upsilamba* was one of Nabokov's fanciful creations, possibly a word he invented out of *upsilon*, the twentieth letter in the Greek alphabet, and *lambda*, the eleventh. So that first day in our private class, we let our minds play again and invented new meanings of our own.

I said I associated *upsilamba* with the impossible joy of a suspended leap. Yassi, who seemed excited for no particular reason, cried out that she always thought it could be the name of a dance—you know, "C'mon, baby, do the Upsilamba with me." I proposed that for the next time, they each write a sentence or two explaining what the word meant to them.

Manna suggested that *upsilamba* evoked the image of small silver fish leaping in and out of a moonlit lake. Nima added in parentheses, Just so you won't forget me, although you have barred me from your class: an upsilamba to you too! For Azin it was a sound, a melody. Mahshid described an image of three girls jumping rope and shouting "Upsilamba!" with each leap. For Sanaz, the word was a small African boy's secret magical name. Mitra wasn't sure why the word reminded her of the paradox of a blissful sigh. And to Nassrin it was the magic code that opened the door to a secret cave filled with treasures.

Upsilamba became part of our increasing repository of coded words and expressions, a repository that grew over time until gradually we had created a secret language of our own. That word became a symbol, a sign of that vague sense of joy, the tingle in the spine Nabokov expected his readers to feel in the act of reading fiction; it was a sensation that separated the good readers, as he called them, from the ordinary ones. It also became the code word that opened the secret cave of remembrance.

Questions for Writing and Discussion

1. Nafisi writes about her assignments, "the most central [question] was how these great works of imagination could help us in our present trapped situation as women." Have you ever used reading or studying as a way to cope with or mentally escape from a difficult situation? How might these strategies be helpful at times when you feel you have little control over a scary situation?

2. In her discussion of *A Thousand and One Nights,* Nafisi mentions that some of the female characters in the novel are silent and therefore "do not quite exist." Discuss a situation in which the choice to be silent made it seem like you, or someone you know, "did not quite exist."

3. All of the girls have a different definition for the made-up word *upsilamba.* What does it mean to you? Use your imagination and try to come up with a definition that isn't the exact definition of any other word you know. After you decide on a definition, use it in a sentence or paragraph and see if others can understand its meaning from the contextual clues you've provided.

4. Have you ever had a private joke or "code word" among friends or family that held special meaning? Write an essay with the word as the title, and, like Nafisi, explain the special meaning and how it came to be.

MAKING IT MATTER

Do you see yourself as a "math person," a "science person," a "humanities person," or someone who excels in another area? How did you come to see yourself this way? What impact do labels like these have on your willingness to face academic challenges in an area that you aren't confident about?

BREAKING IT DOWN

Consider the language and tone that Tobias uses when describing the anxiety some people experience while trying to learn math. What effect does it have on your understanding of how serious a problem math anxiety is?

Symptoms of Math Anxiety
SHEILA TOBIAS

Sheila Tobias has written many books and articles about "neglected issues in science and mathematics education." The following selection is from her book Overcoming Math Anxiety.

◆

The first thing people remember about failing at math is that it felt like sudden death. Whether it happened while learning word problems in sixth grade, coping with equations in high school, or first confronting calculus and statistics in college, failure was instant and frightening. An idea or a new operation was not just difficult, it was impossible! And instead of asking questions or taking the lesson slowly, assuming that in a month or so they would be able to digest it, people remember the feeling, as certain as it was sudden, that they would *never* go any further in mathematics. If we assume, as we must, that the curriculum was reasonable and that the new idea was merely the next in a series of learnable concepts, that feeling of utter defeat was simply not rational; in fact, the autobiographies of math-anxious college students and adults reveal that, no matter how much the teacher reassured them, they sensed that, from that moment on, as far as math was concerned, they were through.

The sameness of that sudden-death experience is evident in the very metaphors people use to describe it. Whether it occurred in elementary school, high school, or college, victims felt that a curtain had been drawn, one they would never see behind, or that there was an impenetrable wall ahead, or that they were at the edge of a cliff, ready to fall off. The most extreme reaction came from a math graduate student. Beginning her dissertation research, she suddenly felt not only that could she never solve her research problem (not unusual in higher mathematics), but that she had never understood advanced math at all. She, too, felt her failure as sudden death.

Paranoia comes quickly on the heels of the anxiety attack. "Everyone knows," the victim believes, "that I don't understand this. The teacher knows. Friends know. I'd better not make it worse by asking questions. Then everyone will find out how dumb I really am." This paranoid reaction is particularly disabling because fear of exposure keeps us from constructive action. We feel guilty and ashamed; not only because our minds seem to have deserted us, but because we believe that our failure to comprehend this one new idea is proof that we have been "faking math" for years.

In a fine analysis of mathophobia, Mitchell Lazarus explains why we feel like frauds. Math failure, he says, passes through a "latency stage" before becoming obvious either to our teachers or to us. It may actually take some time for us to realize that we have been left behind. Lazarus outlines the plight of the high-school student who has always relied on the memorize-what-to-do approach. "Because his grades have been satisfactory, his problem may not be apparent to anyone, including himself. But when his grades finally drop, as they must, even his teachers are unlikely to realize that his problem is not something new, but has been in the making for years."[1]

It is not hard to figure out why failure to understand mathematics can be hidden for so long. Math is usually taught in discrete bits by teachers who were themselves taught this way; students are then tested as they go along. Some of us never get a chance to integrate all these pieces of information, or even to realize what we are not able to do. We are aware of a lack, but though the problem has been building up for years, the first time we are asked to use our knowledge in a new way, it feels like sudden death. It is not so easy to explain, however, why we take such personal responsibility for having "cheated" our teacher, and why

[1]Mitchell Lazarus, "Mathophobia: Some Personal Speculations," Principal Jan-Feb. 1974, p. 18.

so many of us believe that we are frauds. Would we feel the same way if we were floored by irregular verbs in French?

One thing that may contribute to a student's passivity is the fear of making mistakes in mathematics. Teachers, wanting to reward accuracy, go overboard in treating errors as occasions for *shame*, sure to arouse other students' mirth. Successful math students know better. They do not despise their errors. As one math graduate told a surprised group of math-anxious adults, he finds his mistakes "interesting" because they are "windows into my thinking." Eager to avoid errors at all costs, many children never learn how valuable it would be to explore them. Instead, they just sit in the back of the room hoping the teacher will put those flash cards away.

Another source of passivity is a widespread myth—more common in our culture than in others—that mathematical ability is inborn, and that no amount of hard work can possibly compensate for not having a "mathematical mind." Recent studies of *attitudes* toward mathematical competence in elementary-school pupils, their teachers, and their parents to Japan and Taiwan compared with those in the U.S. show how devastating this myth can be. When asked to explain why some children do better in math then others, Asian children, their teachers, and their parents point to *hard work*, their American counterparts to *ability*.[2]

Leaving aside for the moment the source of this myth, consider its effects. Since only a few people are supposed to have a mathematical mind, part of our passive reaction to difficulties in learning mathematics is that we suspect we may not be one of "them" and are waiting for our nonmathematical mind to be exposed. It is only a matter of time before our limit will be reached, so there is not much point in our being methodical or in attending to detail. We are grateful when we survive fractions, word problems, or geometry. If that certain moment of failure hasn't struck yet, it is only temporarily postponed.

Sometimes the math teacher contributes to this myth. If the teacher claims to have had an entirely happy history of learning mathematics, she may contribute to the idea that some people—specifically she—are gifted in mathematics, and others—the students—are not. A good teacher, to allay this myth, brings in the scratch paper he used in working out the problem, to share with the class the many false starts he had to make before solving it.

[2]Harold W. Stevenson and James W. Stigler, The Learning Gap (New York, Summit Books, 1992). See also National Center for Education Statistics, The National Report Card (Washington D.C.: Department of Education, 1992).

Parents, especially parents of girls, often expect their children to be nonmathematical If the parents are poor at math, they had their own sudden-death experience; if math was easy for them, they do not know how it feels to be slow. In either case, they will unwittingly foster the idea that a mathematical mind is something one either has or does not have.

Interestingly, the myth is peculiar to math and science. A teacher of history, for example, is not very likely to tell students that they write poor exams or do badly on papers because they do not have a historical mind. Although we might say that some people have a "feel" for history, the notion that one is *either* historical or nonhistorical is patently absurd. Yet, because even the experts don't *really* know how mathematics is learned, we tend to think of math ability as mystical, and to attribute the talent for it to genetic factors. This belief, though undemonstrable, is clearly communicated to us all.

These considerations help explain why math anxiety afflicts such a wide variety of people having diverse mathematical skills. Since we were never "truly mathematical," we had to memorize things we could not understand. And so, with word problems, or with the first bite of algebra, or at the door of calculus (in some cases, even later), the only way we know how to respond to our failure to understand a difficult concept is to quit. Since we never did have a mathematical mind, our act is over, the curtain down.

Questions for Writing and Discussion

1. List the reasons that Tobias gives for why people suffer from math anxiety. Can you relate to any of the situations that she describes? Do you think the problems she points to are unique to math or have you ever experienced or seen someone else experience these symptoms in other disciplines?

2. One of the problems that Tobias points to is the myth among Americans that math ability is inborn. What do you think about the idea of hard work versus inborn ability? Have you ever cultivated an ability through hard work that you previously considered inborn? If so, describe the situation and what motivated you to work through the challenge. If not, what ability would you like to cultivate and what steps will you need to take in order to achieve this goal?

3. Tobias talks about a mathematics graduate student who finds his mistakes "interesting" because they are a "window into (his) thinking." Have you ever had an insight like this about a mistake you've made? Explain.

4. Write an essay that dispels a commonly held myth about something you know a lot about. Use your experience and knowledge to persuade your reader that your view of this issue is more accurate than the misconception.

MAKING IT MATTER

What differentiates successful students from unsuccessful ones? And how do you measure success?

BREAKING IT DOWN

What do you think the value of beginning a piece of writing with a quiz is? What impact might this activity have on a reader's interest in reading the rest of the selection?

Take This Quiz! (Twenty Reasons You Could Be Working Harder and Longer Than You Have to, Yet Learning Less and Receiving Lower Grades)

ADAM ROBINSON

Adam Robinson graduated from the Wharton School of Business before earning a law degree at Oxford University in England. An author of many books on student success strategies, Robinson has collaborated with the Princeton Review to develop a number of its courses. The following is an excerpt from his book What Smart Students Know: Maximum Grades, Optimum Learning.

◆

IF YOU WANT TO BECOME A SMART STUDENT

You have to see things the way smart students do. . . attitude is the critical difference between smart students and their classmates, and changing your attitude is no easy task.

You may already have the right attitude without realizing it. Or you may feel guilty about that attitude, as if something's wrong with you for having it. We will keep returning to your attitude throughout the book (in periodic *Attitude Checks*), but first let's take a basic inventory.

YOUR INITIAL ATTITUDE INVENTORY

This is just a questionnaire, not a test you're being graded on. It is designed to give you insights into your attitude, so it is crucial that you put down the response that best reflects what you truly think and feel, not what you think is the "right answer." If your opinions have already been influenced by what you've read so far, select the option that best indicates how you felt before you picked up the book.

ATTITUDE CHECK

Instructions: Next to each statement below, put a 1 if you agree with it and a 0 if you disagree. Read each one carefully. These are not trick questions, so take them at face value. This is an important exercise. Don't agonize over your selections, but do give each statement some thought before responding. Take a stand and answer every question.

( ) 1. You are not naturally good at or even interested in learning, so you need to be told by a teacher what to learn and how to learn it.

( ) 2. You cannot be expected to learn on your own or from other students.

( ) 3. You learn in essentially the same way and at the same rate as every other student in your class.

( ) 4. Textbooks are the best resource from which to learn a subject.

( ) 5. Since you are not good at learning, subjects need to be simplified and broken down into a series of skills (tasks, units, objectives) that are presented as drills or workbook exercises. You find such exercises especially rewarding.

( ) 6. Your teacher telling you something is the same thing as teaching it, and you understand that material when you can repeat what the teacher has told you.

( ) 7. The more facts you can repeat, the more you understand.

( ) 8. You would not be interested in learning if you were not "motivated" with rewards like good grades and public praise, or with punishments like bad grades and public criticism.

( ) 9. You would not be interested in learning if you were not tested frequently.

( ) 10. Calling on you randomly in class and expecting an immediate response is a particularly effective teaching method.

( ) 11. Grade competition increases how much you learn and brings out the best in you and your classmates.

( ) 12. If you find, say, history boring, this is because the subject is dull rather than because of the way you are forced to learn it.

( ) 13. There is a certain body of key cultural information that you and everyone else should know; if you do not learn this information by the time you graduate, you never will.

( ) 14. The important information that you need to know is on tests; if something is not on a test, it's not important.

( ) 15. Teachers determine your grades on a consistent, objective basis.

( ) 16. Your marks on tests accurately reflect how well you understand the course subject matter; your grade point average is a good indicator of how much you have learned in the past and how smart you are.

( ) 17. If you listen to what your teachers say and do what your teachers tell you to do, you will learn as much as you are capable of learning.

( ) 18. The faster you learn, the more intelligent you are.

( ) 19. Any learning that takes place in school is a result of your teacher's teaching you; not learning is your fault.

( ) 20. If the way school is run causes you to become confused, discouraged, or rebellious in any way, something is wrong with you.

Add the individual responses to compute your total score. Total Score: The maximum possible score is 20, the minimum is 0. We will discuss this quiz and what your score means . . .

Attitude Shift!

OKAY, LET'S TAKE A LOOK AT THE QUIZ YOU TOOK

1. You are not naturally good at or even interested in learning, so you need to be told by a teacher what to learn and how to learn it.

Jeepers, I hope you disagreed with this one. You learn best from a trained teacher, who should be in total control of the learning process. Sorry, but no teacher knows how you learn best. And you'd better find out quickly if you don't already know!

2. You cannot be expected to learn on your own or from other students.

Smart students strongly disagree with this statement. Before entering school we manage to teach ourselves the fundamentals (with a little coaching from parents). And there's no reason you can't learn as much from your classmates as from your teachers.

3. You learn in essentially the same way and at the same rate as every other student in your class.

Nonsense! Every student learns differently, which is another reason why you and only you know how best to teach yourself.

4. Textbooks are the best resource from which to learn a subject.

Textbooks separate subjects from real life and spoon-feed you isolated and disconnected facts. How many adults do you know who learn their jobs from textbooks?

5. Since you are not good at learning, subjects need to be simplified and broken down into a series of skills (tasks, units, objectives) that are presented as drills or workbook exercises. You find such exercises especially rewarding.

I don't think so. Next.

6. Your teacher telling you something is the same thing as teaching it, and you understand that material when you can repeat what the teacher has told you.

Sorry, but telling you something and having you repeat it does not mean that you understand that material. Don't confuse memorizing with understanding.

7. The more facts you can repeat, the more you understand.

Gong! When was the last time a trivia expert won a Nobel Prize?

8. You would not be interested in learning if you were not "motivated" with rewards like good grades and public praise, or with punishments like bad grades and public criticism.

Take my word for it—you *are* interested in learning. The ever-present threat of bad grades encourages anxiety, not true learning.

9. You would not be interested in learning if you were not tested frequently.

   See my previous comment. Of course you're interested in learning. What you're not interested in is *not* learning, wasting your time, or feeling stupid.

10. Calling on you randomly in class and expecting an immediate response is a particularly effective teaching method.

    Give me a break! This "teaching" method achieves little more than a classroom atmosphere of general panic and possible humiliation. Learning through intimidation? Not interested.

11. Grade competition increases how much you learn and brings out the best in you and your classmates.

    Competition in school is corrosive. It most certainly does not bring out the best in anyone trying to learn. Instead, it creates the impression that learning is worth doing only if you're being graded on it. And since everyone learns at different rates and in different ways, what could grade competition possibly be about? Smart students don't need the spur of grades to make them learn. And ironically, anyone more interested in grades than in learning is going to be beaten in the grade game by someone who's more interested in learning. I can't stress this concept enough.

12. If you find, say, history boring, this is because the subject is dull rather than because of the way you are forced to learn it.

    More likely it's the other way around.

13. There is a certain body of key cultural information that you and everyone else should know; if you do not learn this information by the time you graduate, you never will.

    Who says learning takes place only in school?

14. The important information that you need to know is on tests; if something is not on a test, it's not important.

    Obviously the information you're tested on is important, but tests don't cover everything important in a subject. And they certainly don't cover all the information you need in your life.

15. Teachers determine your grades on a consistent, objective basis.

    No way! Grading couldn't be more inconsistent, subjective, or arbitrary.

16. Your marks on tests accurately reflect how well you under-
    stand the course subject matter; your grade point average is a
    good indicator of how much you have learned in the past and
    how smart you are.

    Schools seem to think so, but I hope you don't. Grading
    is far from being an exact science. Your marks on tests
    reflect a number of things, of which your understanding
    is only one factor; your awareness of what your teacher
    thinks is important also plays an important role.

17. If you listen to what your teachers say and do what your
    teachers tell you to do, you will learn as much as you are ca-
    pable of learning.

    That's a comforting thought, but completely wrong.
    Following orders doesn't guarantee learning.

18. The faster you learn, the more intelligent you are.

    Where was this ever proven? There are sprinters and
    there are marathoners; everyone learns at a different
    pace.

19. Any learning that takes place in school is a result of your
    teacher's teaching you; not learning is your fault.

    Please tell me you disagreed with this one. Students who
    have difficulty learning as school insists everyone learn
    are unfairly labeled lazy, stupid, misbehaved, unmoti-
    vated, or "learning disabled."

20. If the way school is run causes you to become confused, dis-
    couraged, or rebellious in any way, something is wrong with
    you.

    More likely something is wrong with school.

INTERPRETING YOUR "SCORE"

By now you probably realize that the lower your score, the
better. The higher your score, the more you've been brainwashed
by the school system. Not to worry. Together we're going to
change that . . .

If your grand total was a zero, congratulations—yours is the attitude of a smart student. Welcome to the club. But perhaps you
haven't thought of yourself as a smart student. Many potential
smart students have the right attitude about school and the learning process, but they've been made to feel guilty about their
beliefs. Like their classmates, they've been brainwashed by school

to think something is wrong with them, when in fact there's something wrong with school.

WHAT YOU'RE UP AGAINST: HERE'S WHAT SCHOOLS THINK ABOUT *YOU*

You don't acquire your attitude in a vacuum—it's shaped to a large extent by the viewpoint of the school system. This viewpoint is not publicized, but it's not hard to see what it is. To discover how the school system sees *you*—its subject—we should not listen to what it says, but observe what it does. If we take an unflinching look at the typical school experience, if we examine how school is structured, how classes are run and what class time is devoted to, how subjects are taught, what books are used and how they are written, what assignments are given, and what kinds of tests are administered, it becomes very clear how schools view you and your ability to learn.

To find out, simply turn back to the attitude quiz you just took. The purpose of it was to give you a chance to see how much your attitude has been indoctrinated by the school system. **You see, our school system strongly agrees with every one or those statements!**

DOES THAT SURPRISE YOU?

It should. Of course, not all schools or teachers believe all those things about you. If you asked, most teachers would probably deny many of them; some might even be insulted. But while you may not be aware of these institutional attitudes, be assured that they are embodied in our education system.

Unfortunately, you, too, have been conditioned by school and probably share at least some of these beliefs. As a result, you spend more time and energy than you have to, while learning less and receiving lower grades. It is hard to escape their influence because these attitudes are reflected and reinforced in every aspect of school life. Indeed, these notions are so ingrained in the American consciousness that most people have difficulty accepting that they are in fact myths.

THE SMART STUDENT'S CREDO

All smart students, consciously or unconsciously, share twelve beliefs or principles about school and the learning process. Study this list:

Principle #1:	Nobody can teach you as well as you can teach yourself.
Principle #2:	Merely listening to your teachers and completing their assignments is never enough.
Principle #3:	Not everything you are assigned to read or asked to do is equally important.
Principle #4:	Grades are just subjective opinions.
Principle #5:	Making mistakes (and occasionally appearing foolish) is the price you pay for learning and improving.
Principle #6:	The point of a question is to get you to think—*not* simply to answer it.
Principle #7:	You're in school to learn to think for yourself, not to repeat what your textbooks and teachers tell you.
Principle #8:	Subjects do not always seem interesting and relevant, but being actively engaged in learning them is better than being passively bored and not learning them.
Principle #9:	Few things are as potentially difficult, frustrating, or frightening as genuine learning, yet *nothing* is so rewarding and empowering.
Principle #10:	How well you do in school reflects your attitude and your method, not your ability.
Principle #11:	If you're doing it for the grades or for the approval of others, you're missing the satisfactions of the process and putting your self-esteem at the mercy of things outside your control.
Principle #12:	School is a game, but it's a very important game.

You don't have to memorize these principles. (**By the way, there's nothing magical about the number twelve. I just wanted to keep the number of principles manageable**.)

SEEING YOURSELF AS A SMART STUDENT

Taking a look at what amounts to the foundation for a new attitude, you probably notice that these principles reflect not just how you see school and learning, but how you see yourself.

Your self-image has a powerful influence on your academic performance. Aren't all our efforts directed at proving our self-conception? If you see yourself as someone who can't learn, you won't, regardless of the techniques I'm about to show you. Your self-image is crucial to your becoming a smart student, and this is something you have to work out for yourself. If you see yourself as someone who can learn, you will, despite the difficulties you encounter.

The self-image of most students is greatly affected by how well they do at school, which is one of the reasons they find school so difficult. **Paradoxically, the self-image of smart students is not influenced by their performance in school, even though they excel**. Smart students are motivated to learn in spite of—not because of—school. . .

If you want to stop sabotaging yourself and your performance in school, you must first get some idea of what truly makes you tick. I can't change the way you see yourself—you have to do that—but I can change the way you see school.

ONWARD AND UPWARD!

It's not enough for me to tell you what smart students believe. You must accept these things in your heart.

Your attitude has developed over your academic lifetime. It will not change overnight, but the process will pick up momentum the minute you begin. As your attitude begins to change, so will your success in school, which will lead to further changes in your attitude, and still greater achievements.

Questions for Writing and Discussion

1. Robinson writes that "Attitude is the critical difference between smart students and their classmates." To what extent do you agree with Robinson's point? Support your response with evidence from your experience as a student who has known both successful and unsuccessful students.

2. Were you surprised to discover that all of the Attitude Quiz items were false? Which ones surprised you the most? Why? After reading his brief explanation, do you agree with Robinson that all of the items on the quiz were myths? If not, pick one that you question and explain why you wonder about its validity.

3. Choose one of Robinson's 12 principles; attack it or defend it using examples from your own experience or what you have witnessed as a student in the American school system.

4. Robinson implies that grades are more of an impediment to learning than they are helpful. Do you agree with this or do you find grading helpful as a learning tool? Explain your position on the topic in detail.

Making Connections

1. In "How to Say Nothing in 500 Words," Paul Roberts suggests that writers avoid "jargon." What does he mean by *jargon* and how does his point relate to what Amy Tan is saying in "Mother Tongue" (Chapter One) about speaking in front of her readers?

2. A number of selections in this chapter and earlier chapters touch on the role of teachers. Write an essay in which you explain the qualities of an effective or ineffective teacher. Use evidence from the selections in this chapter and/or earlier chapters, as well as your own experience, to make your point.

3. Review paragraphs 21 through 23 of Mike Rose's "I Just Wanna Be Average." To what extent is the experience that Rose describes about trying to solve math problems consistent with what Sheila Tobias describes in "Symptoms of Math Anxiety"?

4. Adam Robinson suggests that the way you see yourself has a powerful impact on your academic performance. Compare Robinson's idea to what Mike Rose ("I Just Wanna Be Average") and Sheila Tobais ("Symptoms of Math Anxiety") are saying. Which similarities are most striking?

5. Mike Rose ("I Just Wanna Be Average"), Azir Nafisi ("Upsilamba!"), and Malcolm X ("Saved," Chapter Three) all discuss situations in which academic study took place outside of a classroom. Compare the experiences these authors describe in unconventional learning environments to what you know and what Adam Robinson suggests about "the classroom." Offer some explanations for these differences as well as some suggestions for how the "classroom experience" could be improved.

Exploring the Web

LD Pride

http://www.ldpride.net
This site, sponsored by the Vancouver Island Invisible Disability Association, was first conceived by Liz Bodog, an adult with learning disabilities. It provides a summary and practical applications of Howard Gardner's theory of multiple intelligences and self-tests for determining one's dominant intelligence and learning style. There is also an explanation of learning styles as well as several links and bulletin boards for discussion of these issues and other disability-related topics.

Emporia State University's Writing Lab

http://www.emporia.edu/writinglab/composition.html
This site features "Composition Corner," which defines the qualities of good writing and provides a number of other practical tips about all stages of the writing process.

Purdue Online Writing Lab

http://owl.english.purdue.edu/
Purdue Online Writing Lab has long been known as a premiere site for up-to-date writing resources, tips, and links.

Mike Rose

http://personalwebs.oakland.edu/~kitchens/rose.html
http://www.mikerosebooks.com/
Both links provide information about Mike Rose, author of "I Just Wanna Be Average." The first includes an excerpt from *Lives on the Boundary* and the other advertises his latest book, *The Mind at Work Valuing the Intelligence of the American Worker*.

"Crossing the Tracks: How 'Untracking' Can Save America's Schools," by Ann Wheelock

http://www.middleweb.com/Whlcktrack.html

"Getting Our Schools on Track: Is Detracking Really the Answer?" by George Ansalone, Ph.D.

http://radicalpedagogy.icaap.org/content/issue6_2/ansalone.html
These two links present opposing viewpoints on the subject of educational tracking.

Azar Nafisi

http://www.identitytheory.com/interviews/birnbaum139.php

http://www.pbs.org/now/transcript/transcript_nafisi.html

Both of these links include interviews with the author about her book
  Reading Lolita in Tehran and about her experiences in postrevolutionary Iran.

The Dialogue Project

http://dialogueproject.sais-jhu.edu/index.php

The website for Dialogue Project, directed by Azar Nafisi, provides a
  "global forum where voices from around the world can meet and
  interact intellectually about the issues that both affect and define
  the relationship between the Islamic world and the West."

How to Study.Org

http://howtostudy.org/

A part of the Chemeketa Community College website, this resource
  offers innumerable links on everything from motivation and
  memory strategies to learning styles and test-taking. It's easy to
  see why over 182 educational institutions link to this site.

Sheila Tobias, *Overcome Math Anxiety* and *Succeed with Math*

http://www.mathanxiety.net/

This link provides information about Sheila Tobias and provides excerpts from her books.

"Math Anxiety"

http://www.lemoyne.edu/academic_advisement/
  academic_support_center/mathanx.htm

LeMoyne College's succinct discussion of and tips for understanding
  and overcoming math anxiety.

Math Anxiety Materials

http://www.ipfw.edu/math/anx_materials.html

This site, part of Indiana–Purdue University at Fort Wayne, provides
  an excellent list of materials, including books, videos, and audio
  cassette tapes, to help students deal with math anxiety.

Becoming an Educated Person: Intellectual Curiosity, Integrity, and Critical Thinking in College and Beyond

Overview

You have a good sense of what it means to be a college student now, but what will this experience do for you as you move through life? The mission of many colleges and universities is not only to help people develop skills that will make them successful in the workforce, but also to assist people in becoming informed, logical, ethical, active, humane, and culturally aware members of society. In short, many institutions of higher learning strive to help their students become educated people.

To what degree do you see this as a goal for your college experience and, perhaps, your life? This chapter presents a variety of perspectives on being and becoming an educated person. It also looks at how striving for this objective can be both satisfying and challenging.

MAKING IT MATTER

How do you approach required courses that are not in your major? Why do you think such courses are required? What value, if any, do you see in these courses?

BREAKING IT DOWN

Weisberger uses traditional essay and paragraph structure to make his point. Identify the topic sentences and supporting evidence in

each body paragraph. To what degree do you think this structure
is effective? Explain.

General Education and a College Degree

RONALD WEISBERGER

*Ronald Weisberger teaches history and a college success course at
Bristol Community College in Fall River, Massachusetts. He is the
coordinator of the Tutoring and Academic Support Center and the
author of many articles on issues relevant to higher education. This
selection originally appeared in* College Success Seminar: Strategies
for Building College Skills.

✦

There are at least two basic reasons for seeking a college degree.
The first is to gain the necessary skills to pursue a satisfying
career. Whether the career is in business, the health professions
or the government, there are knowledge and skills that must be
obtained in order to achieve a certain level of proficiency. The
other reason is to gain a greater understanding of oneself and the
world. It is this second area that is dealt with in what colleges
refer to as general, or liberal arts, education.

A general, or liberal arts, education covers the major areas of
knowledge including the humanities, social sciences, and natural
sciences. These academic fields provide us with perspectives on
who we are as human beings, why we act as we do, and the nature of the world and the universe in which we live. These are
broad fields and are broken down into smaller areas. For example, the humanities include the study of specific languages, history,
literature, philosophy, art, and music; the social sciences include
psychology, sociology, political science, economics, and anthro-
pology; and the natural sciences include biology, chemistry,
physics, astronomy, and geology. Students who want to pursue
particular areas in depth can eventually major in one or more of
these subject areas. However, the purpose of general education
is to provide students with an overall view of these spheres of

knowledge and gain an appreciation for the ways in which specialists pursue and enlarge our understanding of the world and ourselves.

Students sometimes wonder why they have to spend time taking courses in the areas mentioned when they are interested in becoming an accountant, engineer, math teacher, or dental hygienist? The answer is that, traditionally, going to college has meant more than just pursuing a career. Rather, it has involved striving to become a more educated person. In order to do so, it is necessary to at least be aware of the areas of knowledge mentioned. More importantly, being introduced to subjects in the humanities and the natural and social sciences can enrich a person's life and set him/her on the path to being a life-long learner.

There are also practical reasons for pursuing courses of a general nature. A general, or liberal arts education can improve a person's communication and critical-thinking skills. It is these skills that employers say they are looking for when hiring new personnel. Many CEOs of major corporations, for example, were themselves history, philosophy, or science majors. They point out that they prefer to hire employees who have been exposed to the liberal arts because it means that they tend to be more flexible and open to new ideas. In a society that is constantly changing, the liberal arts can help a person adjust to new environments. This is very important both in a particular job or when looking for new jobs since it is rare these days for a person to keep the same position throughout his/her working career.

Another essential reason for being exposed to the liberal arts is the necessity of being able to live in a multicultural nation and world. A general education introduces students to a variety of cultures and also helps them to see how our society and world civilization, in general, have evolved. This background can help in adjusting to changes in a particular society and the world. An understanding of the liberal arts is particularly important in a democratic society where citizens are called upon to make crucial decisions as to who they want to have as representatives on the national and world scene. In addition, in a world where there is much conflict and strife, a liberal arts education can help us to better understand those people who may be different and assist in creating greater understanding and tolerance among people.

Finally, general and liberal arts can help in one's personal life. Becoming a spouse or partner, as well as becoming a parent, calls for a better understanding of how to play these essential roles in life. Courses in, for example, psychology, literature, or biology can provide important information and knowledge that allow a person to grow both mentally and physically. This knowledge can also help significant others do the same.

Questions for Discussion and Writing

1. Do you agree with the thesis of this article? Write a response to this article that argues for or against the points made here. Use Weisberger's essay as a model for how to structure your piece.

2. Weisberger states that there are "two basic reasons for seeking a college degree." What is your primary reason for seeking a degree? Is it one that Weisberger mentions or is it something he doesn't discuss? To what extent do you find this reason motivational?

3. Interview some faculty members, family members, friends, professionals in the field you are pursuing, and others in the community about the value of a liberal education. How do these perspectives compare with your view and the author's view? What, if anything, did you learn from your research?

4. Have you ever taken a course that taught you something you did not anticipate when you enrolled in the course? For example, maybe you took a statistics course that taught you to be organized in your note-taking or a public speaking course that made you more aware of cultural differences. Write an essay that explains how you learned an unanticipated skill or gained an unexpected level of awareness as a result of taking a particular course.

MAKING IT MATTER

When you think about your life over the next 20 or more years, what role do you see education playing in your life? Explain your perspective and what led you to it.

BREAKING IT DOWN

Who is the intended audience for this article? Where in the article does the tone and purpose shift, revealing this intended audience? What impact does the shift have on you as a reader?

The Nontraditional Student in You
MICHELE COMPTON AND CANDY SCHOCK

Michele Compton and Candy Schock wrote this article for Women in Business, *where it first appeared in 2000.*

———————— ✦ ————————

As the baby boomers hit middle age, many of them are opting to go back to school in droves. In 1984, more than 23 million Americans were involved in adult education, according to the National Center for Education Statistics. That number then rose to 76 million in 1995, and some anticipate it will reach to more than 100 million by 2004. Why the sudden interest in continuing education? Everything from career advancement to divorce can trigger the response to return to the classroom.

As nontraditional students, the decision to begin or finish an advanced education program is not one taken lightly, especially by women. With the term "nontraditional" comes many decisions and responsibilities, including choosing a college, negotiating tuition costs and balancing a career, family and classwork. Despite these and other obstacles, the statistics hold true. People across the country are not only returning to school—they're walking away with the degree of their dreams.

THE RE-EDUCATED GENERATION

Typically, a nontraditional student is defined as 25 years of age or older. According to the Digest of Education Statistics, the number of students over the age of 30 has risen by more than a million in the past 10 years alone. Higher education enrollment statistics also point out that the largest percentage of students during the past decade were women.

But there is no one description that fits all those returning to school. It may have been five years or several decades since you last stepped foot on a college campus. You may be pursuing a degree, advanced training for career development or simply heading back to school to learn more about your area of interest.

While historically an advanced degree has been equated with success, many professionals are finding that their careers are changing and they need the educational support to succeed in an entirely new field. Mary M. Witherspoon, a member of North Dallas Chapter and 1998 national president, went back to school to change careers. After 14 years as a certified public accountant in the oil industry, she enjoyed her public speaking and seminar work with ABWA and decided to switch careers to instructional design. "I took the severance package my company offered me, and went back to school to get my master's degree," she says. "Age has nothing to do with learning. When you are ready to learn, you can do so." Mary attended Amber University in Garland, Texas, where she earned her master's degree in human resources and training, and graduated with a 4.0 grade point average.

While Mary's situation may be atypical for nontraditional students, many career-savvy women are realizing they need to continue their education after they have found their career of choice. Alice Allen, a member of Flower City Chapter in Rochester, N.Y., received her bachelor's in nursing education and began working as a nurse. However, when her family situation changed because of divorce, she forced herself to look realistically at the job market and saw the writing on the wall. "I wanted to remain up-to-date in my field," she says. "And I felt the future required an advanced education. Also, since I was suddenly single, I needed a way to adequately support my children." Alice went back to school at the University of Rochester in Rochester, N.Y. She finished her master's degree and became a clinical nurse specialist.

A similar reason took Louise Worshon back to school. "When I attended an ABWA meeting, I felt the speaker was talking directly to me," says Louise, a member of Day Timers Chapter in the Jacksonville, Fla. "I needed more education than a high school diploma to succeed in the trust department of the bank where I worked. The next day I asked my boss about going back to school to receive a trust certificate and, much to my delight, he said yes."

THE EDUCATION QUESTION

Once you've made the decision to turn your attention to the classroom, you may be wondering where to go to school. There are many factors to consider when choosing a college or university. With a broad range of choices, you must look carefully at your degree requirements in order to ensure the school meets all your expectations.

Location also is important. When Louise discussed the trust certificate program with her boss, he agreed to pay the tuition and mileage for the 100-mile round-trip to the University of Florida.

And what about cost? During the 1998–99 academic year, reports showed the average annual price for tuition and expenses at a public college was estimated at $7,000. Private colleges averaged $19,000 a year.

Fortunately, today's nontraditional students have several advantages. As established professionals, many students are able to pay portions or all of their own tuition and rely on grants or loans for the remainder.

The lifelong learning ambition of employees also is a habit many companies want to foster. Check with your company to see whether you can take advantage of a tuition-reimbursement plan.

In addition to her severance pay, Mary also benefited from the Stephen Button Memorial Educational Fund's financial aid package. "ABWA has awarded more than $13 million in financial aid since 1980," she says. "I received my aid in the form of an interest-free loan and a grant. The Association was an invaluable partner to my success in obtaining an advanced degree."

There are other routes to follow, too. State and government agencies offer a variety of financial aid packages designed for levels of income and degree ambition. Also, the number of scholarships and fellowships available have been rising steadily in past years. Alice received government-sponsored Federal Traineeship tuition assistance through the University of Buffalo in New York. Check with the financial aid department of your school of choice for more information on the options.

THE EDUCATED FAMILY

While advancing your education is a positive and life-changing step, very few people are in a position to quit their jobs and attend school full time. Most nontraditional students are familiar with the delicate balance among family responsibilities, work schedules and the academic calendar. Careful planning may be your best ally. Begin by explaining to your family why you are going back to school and the rewards and benefits of your choice. Explain how important this is to you, then enlist their support. Be honest about how your additional time away from home may affect them and what tasks they may need to do. Ask them to pitch in.

Alice was careful to make a point of explaining her decision to her family. "The children sometimes resented my time away from home as I worked toward my master's," Alice says. "But I explained to them that I needed to further my education to support them and provide for their future education as well. Now as adults, they tell me they are glad I overcame their concerns and returned to school."

Alice recommends keeping younger children busy with sports, camps and church activities. This will help occupy your children's attention while you are gone and makes the time spent apart go faster for them. Overall, only you can decide if your family can weather the changes your return to school will necessitate.

While juggling family, work and school is seldom easy, it can be done. It might help to remember that your classes will likely revolve around your skills or interests so they will be less burdensome. Your work experience also will be instrumental in helping you stay focused, organized and ready to reach your goal. Also, in light of the increase in nontraditional student enrollment, colleges and universities are moving full steam ahead to help meet the time constraints these students face. Night classes, online courses or Saturday sessions may be available at your school of choice.

THE EDUCATION ADVANTAGE

Advancing your education is always a return on your investment. Companies value education. If you went back to school to further your education in your field, chances are good that you will see an increase in salary.

After Louise graduated, she received many job offers—some from across the country. She chose to remain in her current position where she tripled her salary in a year's time. When a new trust department division opened, Louise was asked to manage it. "I was the first woman to complete the Trust Certificate program, and going back to school for the training was the best thing that could have happened to my banking career," she says. "A real perk was that my employer paid for me to attend the National Association of Bank Women's conventions and ABWA's national conventions."

Whatever your expectations, there is an immense sense of satisfaction when you are finished. It's a moment in your career where you can reflect on how far you've come and how far you can go.

Questions for Writing and Discussion

1. Attack or defend the following quotation by Mary M. Witherspoon: "Age has nothing to do with learning. When you are ready to learn, you can do so." Use examples from your own experience to make your point and consider other variables, besides age, that might influence one's readiness to be a successful college student.

2. Are the students in your classes more or less diverse in terms of life experience than you expected? What impact, if any, has this level of classroom diversity had on your experience so far? Explain.

3. Compton and Schock close their article with the following point about returning to school: "Whatever your expectations, there is an immense sense of satisfaction when you are finished." Write about an experience you had that provided you with "an immense sense of satisfaction." Why do you think this experience was so satisfying? What did you learn about yourself in this situation that might lead to more satisfaction in the future?

4. Think about someone you know who might benefit from returning to school for personal or professional reasons. Write that person a letter detailing the reasons he or she should continue his or her education. Use evidence from this article and other sources, if necessary, to strengthen your argument.

MAKING IT MATTER

What role do you think service learning has in a college curriculum? Should students be required to participate in community service projects as part of a degree or certificate program? Why or why not?

BREAKING IT DOWN

Overholt opens and closes with the image of a specific child. Do you find this strategy effective? Why or why not?

Vamos a Leer!

RIA OVERHOLT

As a student at Western Montana College of the University of Montana, Ria Overholt participated in Vamos a Leer, *a community service project under the Montana Campus Compact. She was also the recipient of that organization's Outstanding Service Project Award in 2001. This selection originally appeared in a book of collected works by Montana Campus Compact participants entitled* Study Groups, Sacrifices and Strong Coffee: Engaged College Students Share Their Stories.

———————— ✦ ————————

There is a picture hanging on my refrigerator of a little boy's dark-haired head bent over a book. This picture means so much to me because it symbolizes an accomplishment. It is an accomplishment that the majority of us will never achieve: the mastery of a second language. This little first-grade boy, Carlos (not his real name), learned the English language, not out of desire but necessity. His parents had moved to America from Mexico two years prior, to find "the American Dream" and a higher quality of life. That path led them to a little ranch outside of Dillon, Montana where the father labors long hours at minimum pay to provide the family with a home in a tiny trailer perched on the side of a sagebrush hill. Inside the trailer, Carlos and his sister share a room in which the few toys leave little room for the sister's bed on the floor. Carlos entered kindergarten not knowing a word of English. Through the help of his teachers and a woman funded by a Migrant Children's Fund, he was able to learn to speak English. Reading the language was more difficult, though. Without strong support from home, he was not progressing at the rate of the other students in his class. This is where the idea for the project, Vamos a Leer, sprang from.

Vamos a Leer was the brainchild of Jeanna Meier-Francisconi. She identified the need in the community, and I was fortunate to be able to help her implement the program. We spent the first semester making contacts and asking questions. When working with minority groups, it seems as if everyone is willing to admit that there is a need, but no one is sure how to address that need. There is a Migrant Children's Fund in Dillon that is focused on providing in-school assistance and home visits to the families. We felt that we could supplement that and provide after-school tutorials that would bring Western Montana College and the local school systems together in a synergistic relationship.

Western Montana College prides itself on having a strong teacher education program. Our hope was that we could help Western provide a stronger diversity experience for its students while filling our need for educated tutors. Persevering through extensive communications and initial planning, we were able to begin working with two professors on campus who taught reading diagnostic classes. As part of their curriculum, they required of their students a certain amount of tutoring hours each semester. We matched up some of these college students with our Hispanic children in the fall of 1999.

The program continues to grow every year with added refinements being implemented as needed. At times we had enormous obstacles such as transportation and language barriers placed before us, but we always managed to overcome them. The real motivational factor for us was the enjoyment of working with the children and their families.

When we first started working with this project, we attended a meeting with all of the Hispanic families in the community. They were so excited by our willingness to help their children. Since then we have had numerous home visits with them and extensive contact. The home visits are always a joy because they usually feed us authentic Mexican cuisine! (Take all ideas of food you have received in restaurants and throw them out the window, because this food is like nothing you have ever tasted before.) I have fallen in love with every one of the children. They trust me and look to me for guidance. We have a little third-grade boy who hugs me every time he sees me. There is one family that had a baby at the same time that I had mine. We exchange gifts and advice on a regular basis. The families are what make this project a success.

I started working with AmeriCorps with the idea of "effectively doing my job" for two years and then moving on. I cannot walk away from it now. Little Carlos has become my motivator and my inspiration. While he is still not reading quite up to grade level, he has shown dramatic improvement. The most wonderful part, though, is that he is now excited about reading. I feel that is our ultimate success. For the past three years I have been working to receive my degree in Geology. Because of Carlos and all of my wonderful experiences these past few years, I am planning on changing my major and pursuing a degree in the Social Sciences. Now that I have begun to help people, I do not ever want to stop.

Questions for Writing and Discussion

1. Describe a task that you undertook because it was required of you that turned out to be more rewarding than you expected.

2. Overholt opens with an image of Carlos that she says "symbolizes an accomplishment." Choose a photograph or mental image that you cherish and write an essay about what it symbolizes for you.

3. Identify a need in your community or a community that you are familiar with. What could students at your college do to serve this community need? How might this relationship serve students as well?

4. Many people believe that contributing to their community is a great thing to do, but obstacles such as lack of time often prevent people from getting involved. Are there obstacles that prevent you from participating in a program like Vamos a Leer? What could you do to overcome these obstacles?

MAKING IT MATTER

When you do research online, how do you know that the information you are finding is accurate?

BREAKING IT DOWN

Seigenthaler provides details about the process he underwent to find his "biographer." How does allowing the reader into this process, rather than just revealing what he discovered, strengthen his thesis?

A False Wikipedia "Biography"
JOHN SEIGENTHALER

John Seigenthaler is a retired journalist who founded The Freedom Forum First Amendment Center at Vanderbilt University. This editorial first appeared on USA Today.com.

"John Seigenthaler Sr. was the assistant to Attorney General Robert Kennedy in the early 1960's. For a brief time, he was thought to have been directly involved in the Kennedy assassinations of both John, and his brother, Bobby. Nothing was ever proven."
—Wikipedia

——————— ✦ ———————

This is a highly personal story about Internet character assassination. It could be your story.

I have no idea whose sick mind conceived the false, malicious "biography" that appeared under my name for 132 days on Wikipedia, the popular, online, free encyclopedia whose authors are unknown and virtually untraceable. There was more:

"John Seigenthaler moved to the Soviet Union in 1971, and returned to the United States in 1984," Wikipedia said. "He started one of the country's largest public relations firms shortly thereafter."

At age 78, I thought I was beyond surprise or hurt at anything negative said about me. I was wrong. One sentence in the biography was true. I was Robert Kennedy's administrative assistant in the early 1960s. I also was his pallbearer. It was mind-boggling when my son, John Seigenthaler, journalist with NBC News, phoned later to say he found the same scurrilous text on Reference.com and Answers.com.

I had heard for weeks from teachers, journalists and historians about "the wonderful world of Wikipedia," where millions of people worldwide visit daily for quick reference "facts," composed and posted by people with no special expertise or knowledge—and sometimes by people with malice.

At my request, executives of the three websites now have removed the false content about me. But they don't know, and can't find out, who wrote the toxic sentences.

ANONYMOUS AUTHOR

I phoned Jimmy Wales, Wikipedia's founder and asked, "Do you . . . have any way to know who wrote that?"

"No, we don't," he said. Representatives of the other two websites said their computers are programmed to copy data verbatim from Wikipedia, never checking whether it is false or factual.

Naturally, I want to unmask my "biographer." And, I am interested in letting many people know that Wikipedia is a flawed and irresponsible research tool.

But searching cyberspace for the identity of people who post spurious information can be frustrating. I found on Wikipedia the registered IP (Internet Protocol) number of my "biographer"—65-81-97-208. I traced it to a customer of BellSouth Internet. That company advertises a phone number to report "Abuse Issues." An electronic voice said all complaints must be e-mailed. My two e-mails were answered by identical form letters, advising me that the company would conduct an investigation but might not tell me the results. It was signed "Abuse Team."

Wales, Wikipedia's founder, told me that BellSouth would not be helpful. "We have trouble with people posting abusive things over and over and over," he said. "We block their IP numbers, and they sneak in another way. So we contact the service providers, and they are not very responsive."

After three weeks, hearing nothing further about the Abuse Team investigation, I phoned BellSouth's Atlanta corporate headquarters, which led to conversations between my lawyer and BellSouth's counsel. My only remote chance of getting the name, I learned, was to file a "John or Jane Doe" lawsuit against my "biographer." Major communications Internet companies are bound by federal privacy laws that protect the identity of their customers, even those who defame online. Only if a lawsuit resulted in a court subpoena would BellSouth give up the name.

LITTLE LEGAL RECOURSE

Federal law also protects online corporations—BellSouth, AOL, MCI Wikipedia, etc.—from libel lawsuits. Section 230 of the Communications Decency Act, passed in 1996, specifically states that "no provider or user of an interactive computer service shall be treated as the publisher or speaker." That legalese means that, unlike print and broadcast companies, online service providers cannot be sued for disseminating defamatory attacks on citizens posted by others.

Recent low-profile court decisions document that Congress effectively has barred defamation in cyberspace. Wikipedia's website acknowledges that it is not responsible for inaccurate information, but Wales, in a recent C-Span interview with Brian

Lamb, insisted that his website is accountable and that his community of thousands of volunteer editors (he said he has only one paid employee) corrects mistakes within minutes.

My experience refutes that. My "biography" was posted May 26. On May 29, one of Wales' volunteers "edited" it only by correcting the misspelling of the word "early." For four months, Wikipedia depicted me as a suspected assassin before Wales erased it from his website's history Oct. 5. The falsehoods remained on Answers.com and Reference.com for three more weeks.

In the C-Span interview, Wales said Wikipedia has "millions" of daily global visitors and is one of the world's busiest websites. His volunteer community runs the Wikipedia operation, he said. He funds his website through a non-profit foundation and estimated a 2006 budget of "about a million dollars."

And so we live in a universe of new media with phenomenal opportunities for worldwide communications and research—but populated by volunteer vandals with poison-pen intellects. Congress has enabled them and protects them.

When I was a child, my mother lectured me on the evils of "gossip." She held a feather pillow and said, "If I tear this open, the feathers will fly to the four winds, and I could never get them back in the pillow. That's how it is when you spread mean things about people."

For me, that pillow is a metaphor for Wikipedia.

Questions for Writing and Discussion

1. Discuss a situation in which you were unfairly or inaccurately portrayed. How did you deal with the situation? What did you take away from the experience?

2. Seigenthaler explains that "unlike print and broadcast companies, online service providers cannot be sued for disseminating defamatory attacks on citizens posted by others." Do you agree with the author that this law should be changed, or do you support this legislation? Explain.

3. Go to your college's library, writing lab, or academic support center (or the website for one of these services at your college) and ask for information about evaluating online sources. Use this information to evaluate one of the websites in the Exploring the Web section of this chapter.

4. If you feel strongly about the value of "a community of editors," an idea that is central to the success of wikis such as Wikipedia, write an editorial that responds to Seigenthaler and explains why, despite what happened to him, wikis are valuable to researchers.

MAKING IT MATTER

Do you consider yourself an ambitious person? What limits have you placed on the goals and dreams you have for yourself?

BREAKING IT DOWN

Consider the details that Klass chooses to support her point. Why do you think she uses both examples from her personal experience and from the larger culture to develop her argument?

Ambition
PERRI KLASS

Perri Klass is a professional writer of fiction and nonfiction as well as a pediatrician.

———————— ✦ ————————

In college, my friend Beth was very ambitious, not only for herself but for her friends. She was interested in foreign relations, in travel, in going to law school. . . . I was a biology major, which was a problem: Beth's best friend from childhood was also studying biology, and Beth had already decided *she* would win the Nobel Prize. This was resolved by my interest in writing fiction. I would win *that* Nobel, while her other friend would win for science.

It was a joke; we were all smart-ass college freshmen, pretending the world was ours for the asking. But it was not entirely a joke. We were *smart* college freshmen, and why should we limit our ambitions?

I've always liked ambitious people, and many of my closest friends have had grandiose dreams. I like such people, not because I am desperate to be buddies with a future secretary of state but because I find ambitious people entertaining, interesting to talk to, fun to watch. And, of course, I like such people because I am ambitious myself, and I would rather not feel apologetic about it.

Ambition has gotten bad press. Back in the seventeenth century, Spinoza thought ambition and lust were "nothing but species

of madness, although they are not enumerated among diseases."
Especially in women, ambition has often been seen as a pro-
foundly dislikable quality; the word "ambitious" linked to a "career
woman" suggested that she was ruthless, hard as nails, clawing
her way to success on top of bleeding bodies of her friends.

Then, in the late Seventies and the Eighties, ambition became
desirable, as books with titles like *How to Stomp Your Way to
Success* became bestsellers. It was still a nasty sort of attribute,
but nasty attributes were good because they helped you look out
for number one.

But what I mean by ambition is dreaming big dreams, putting no limits on your expectations and your hopes. I don't really
like very specific, attainable ambitions, the kind you learn to set
in the career-strategy course taught by the author of *How to
Stomp Your Way to Success.* I like big ambitions that suggest that
the world could open up at any time, with work and luck and de-
termination. The next book could hit it big. The next research
project could lead to something fantastic. The next bright idea
could change history.

Of course, eventually you have to stop being a freshman in
college. You limit your ambitions and become more realistic,
wiser about your potential, your abilities, the number of things
your life can hold. Sometimes you get close to something you
wanted to do, only to find it looks better from far away. Back
when I was a freshman, to tell the truth, I wanted to be Jane
Goodall, go into the jungle to study monkeys and learn things no
one had ever dreamed of. This ambition was based on an interest
in biology and several *National Geographic* television specials; it
turned out that wasn't enough of a basis for a life. There were a
number of other early ambitions that didn't pan out either. I was
not fated to live a wild, adventurous life, to travel alone to all the
most exotic parts of the world, to leave behind a string of broken
hearts. Oh well, you have to grow up, at least a little.

One of the worst things ambition can do is tell you you're a
failure. The world is full of measuring tapes, books and articles to
tell you where you should be at your age, after so-and-so many
years of doing what you do. . . .

The world is full of disappointed people. Some of them probably never had much ambition to start with; they sat back and
waited for something good and feel cheated because it never happened. Some of them had very set, specific ambitions and, for one

reason or another, never got what they wanted. Others got what they wanted but found it wasn't exactly what they'd expected it to be. Disappointed ambition provides fodder for both drama and melodrama: aspiring athletes (who coulda been contenders), aspiring dancers (all they ever needed was the music and the mirror).

The world is also full of people so ambitious, so consumed by drive and overdrive that nothing they pass on the way to success has any value at all. Life becomes one long exercise in delayed gratification; everything you do, you're doing only because it will one day get you where you want to be. Medical training is an excellent example of delayed gratification. You spend years in medical school doing things with no obvious relationship to your future as a doctor, and then you spend years in residency, living life on a miserable schedule, staying up all night and slogging through the day, telling yourself that one day all this will be over. . . .

As you grow up, your ambitions may come into conflict. Most prominently nowadays, we have to hear about Women Torn Between Family and Career, about women who make it to the top only to realize they left their ovaries behind. Part of growing up, of course, is realizing that there is only so much room in one life, whether you are male or female. You can do one thing whole-heartedly and single-mindedly and give up some other things. Or you can be greedy and grab for something new without wanting to give up what you already have. This leads to a chaotic and crowded life in which you are always late, always overdue, always behind, but rarely bored. Even so, you have to come to terms with limitations; you cannot crowd your life with occupations and then expect to do each one as well as you might if it were all you had to do. I realize this when I race out of the hospital, offending a senior doctor who had offered to explain something to me, only to arrive late at the daycare center, annoying the people who have been taking care of my daughter.

People consumed by ambition, living with ambition, get to be a little humorless, a little one-sided. On the other hand, people who completely abrogate their ambition aren't all fun and games either. I've met a certain number of women whose ambitions are no longer for themselves at all; their lives are now dedicated to their offspring. I hope my children grow up to be nice people, smart people, people who use good grammar; and I hope they grow up to find things they love to do, and do well. But my ambitions are for *me*.

Of course, I try to be mature about it all. I don't assign my friends Nobel Prizes or top government posts. I don't pretend that there is room in my life for any and every kind of ambition I can imagine. Instead, I say piously that all I want are three things: I want to write as well as I can, I want to have a family and I want to be a good pediatrician. And then, of course, a voice inside whispers . . . to write a bestseller, to have ten children, to do stunning medical research. Fame and fortune, it whispers, fame and fortune. Even though I'm not a college freshman anymore, I'm glad to find that little voice still there, whispering sweet nothings in my ear.

Questions for Writing and Discussion

1. If someone called you *ambitious*, would you take this as a compliment or an insult? Do you think there is truth to what Klass is saying about the "bad press" that ambition has gotten, especially in terms of how it is used when talking about women?

2. Compare the ambitions you have today to those you had as a child. How have they changed? How have they remained the same? To what do you attribute these similarities and differences?

3. What point is Klass making about ambition? Do you agree with her point? How has your level of ambition affected your life?

4. Klass sees advantages and disadvantages to being ambitious, but comes to a compromise in order to define the term in her conclusion. Write an essay about something that you feel ambivalent about. Did the act of writing help you clarify your position?

MAKING IT MATTER

When you think of your life after college, what do you imagine? How will it be similar to your life today? How do you expect it to be different?

BREAKING IT DOWN

The following selection is the first chapter of *Quarterlife Crisis: The Unique Challenges of Life in Your Twenties* (2001). As you read this selection, ask yourself what the authors' goals were for the first chapter. Do you think they achieved their purpose?

What Is the Quarterlife Crisis?

ALEXANDRA ROBBINS AND ABBY WILNER

Alexandra Robbinson and Abby Wilner wrote Quarterlife Crisis: The Unique Challenges of Life in Your Twenties *(2001). They based this book on their own experiences after college and on interviews with hundreds of other people in their 20s. The following selection is excerpted from the book's introduction.*

———————————— ✦ ————————————

Jim, the neighbor who lives in the three-story colonial down the block, has recently turned 50. You know this because Jim's wife threw him a surprise party about a month ago. You also know this because, since then, Jim has dyed his hair blond, purchased a leather bomber jacket, traded in his Chevy Suburban for a sleek Miata, and ditched the wife for a girlfriend half her size and age.

Yet, aside from the local ladies' group's sympathetic clucks for the scorned wife, few neighbors are surprised at Jim's instant lifestyle change. Instead, they nod their heads understandingly. "Oh, Jim," they say. "He's just going through a midlife crisis. Everyone goes through it." Friends, colleagues, and family members excuse his weird behavior as an inevitable effect of reaching this particular stage of life. Like millions of other middle-aged people, Jim has reached a period during which he believes he must ponder the direction of his life—and then alter it.

Chances are . . . you're not Jim. You know this because you can't afford a leather bomber jacket, you drive your parents' Volvo (if you drive a car at all), and, regardless of your gender, you would happily marry Jim's wife if she gets to keep the house. But Jim's midlife crisis is relevant to you nonetheless, because it is currently the only age-related crisis that is widely recognized as a common, inevitable part of life. This is pertinent because, despite all of the attention lavished on the midlife crisis, despite the hundreds of books, movies, and magazine articles dedicated to explaining the sometimes traumatic transition through middle age and the ways to cope with it, the midlife crisis is not the only age-related crisis that we experience. As Yoda whispered to Luke Skywalker, "There is another."

This other crisis can be just as, if not more, devastating than the midlife crisis. It can throw someone's life into chaotic disarray or paralyze it completely. It may be the single most concentrated period during which individuals relentlessly question their future and how it will follow the events of their past. It covers the interval that encompasses the transition from the academic world to the "real" world—an age group that can range from late adolescence to the mid-thirties but is usually most intense in twenty somethings. It is what we call the quarterlife crisis, and it is a real phenomenon.

The quarterlife crisis and the midlife crisis stem from the same basic problem, but the resulting panic couldn't be more opposite. At their cores, both the quarterlife and the midlife crisis are about a major life change. Often, for people experiencing a midlife crisis, a sense of stagnancy sparks the need for change. During this period, a middle-aged person tends to reflect on his past, in part to see if his life to date measures up to the life he had envisioned as a child (or as a twentysomething). The midlife crisis also impels a middle-aged person to look forward, sometimes with an increasing sense of desperation, at the time he feels he has left.

In contrast, the quarterlife crisis occurs precisely because there is none of that predictable stability that drives middle-aged people to do unpredictable things. After about twenty years in a sheltered school setting—or more if a person has gone on to graduate or professional school—many graduates undergo some sort of culture shock. In the academic environment, goals were clear-cut and the ways to achieve them were mapped out distinctly. To get into a good college or graduate school, it helped if you graduated with honors; to graduate with honors, you needed to get good grades; to get good grades, you had to study hard. If your goals were athletic, you worked your way up from junior varsity or walk-on to varsity by practicing skills, working out in the weight room, and gelling with teammates and coaches. The better you were, the more playing time you got, the more impressive your statistics could become.

But after graduation, the pathways blur. In that crazy, wild nexus that people like to call the "real world," there is no definitive way to get from point A to point B, regardless of whether the points are related to a career, financial situation, home, or social life (though we have found through several unscientific studies that offering to pay for the next round of drinks can usually improve three out of the four). The extreme uncertainty that twenty somethings experience after graduation occurs because what was once a solid line that they could follow throughout their series of educational institutions has now disintegrated into millions of different options. The sheer number of possibilities can certainly inspire hope—that is why people say that twentysomethings have their whole lives ahead of them. But the endless array of decisions can also make a recent graduate feel utterly lost.

So while the midlife crisis revolves around a doomed sense of stagnancy, of a life set on pause while the rest of the world rattles on, the quarterlife crisis is a response to overwhelming instability, constant change, too many choices, and a panicked sense of helplessness. Just as the monotony of a lifestyle stuck in idle can drive a person to question himself intently, so, too, can the uncertainty of a life thrust into chaos. The transition from childhood to adulthood—from school to the world beyond—comes as a jolt for which many of today's twentysomethings simply are not prepared. The resulting overwhelming senses of helplessness and cluelessness, of indecision and apprehension, make up the real and common experience we call the quarterlife crisis. Individuals who are approaching middle age at least know what is coming. Because the midlife crisis is so widely acknowledged, people who undergo it are at the very least aware that there are places where they can go for help, such as support groups, books, movies, or Internet sites. Twentysomethings, by contrast, face a crisis that hits them with a far more powerful force than they ever expected. The slam is particularly painful because today's twentysomethings believe that they are alone and that they are having a much more difficult transition period than their peers—because the twenties are supposed to be "easy," because no one talks about these problems, and because the difficulties are therefore so unexpected. And at the fragile, doubt-ridden age during which the quarterlife crisis occurs, the ramifications can be extremely dangerous.

WHY WORRY ABOUT A QUARTERLIFE CRISIS?

The whirlwind of new responsibilities, new liberties, and new choices can be entirely overwhelming for someone who has just emerged from the shelter of twenty years of schooling. We don't mean to make graduates sound as if they have been hibernating since they emerged from the womb; certainly it is not as if they have been slumbering throughout adolescence (though some probably tried). They have in a sense, however, been encased in a bit of a cocoon, where someone or something—parents or school, for example—has protected them from a lot of the scariness of their surroundings. As a result, when graduates are let loose into the world, their dreams and desires can be tinged with trepidation. They are hopeful, but at the same time they are also, to put it simply, scared silly.

Some might say that because people have had to deal with the rite of passage from youth to adulthood since the beginning of time, this crisis is not really a "crisis" at all, given that historically this transitional period has, at various times, been marked with ceremonial rituals involving things like spears and buffalo dung. Indeed, it may not always have been a crisis.

But it has become one.

Maybe it is because the career and financial opportunities for college graduates have skyrocketed in the past decade and, therefore, so has the pressure to succeed. Maybe it is because the crazy people out there who amuse themselves by going on shooting rampages seem to have proliferated in recent years, leaving young adults more fearful of entering into relationships with new friends, lovers, and roommates. Or maybe increasing competition from the rising millions of fellow students has left twentysomethings feeling like they have to work harder than ever to stand out from their peers. Whatever the reason, the quarterlife crisis poses enough of a threat to the well-being of many graduates—however well-adjusted they may be—that it has to be taken seriously. Here's why.

Although hope is a common emotion for twentysomethings, hopelessness has become just as widespread. The revelation that life simply isn't easy—a given for some twentysomethings, a mild inconvenience for others, but a shattering blow for several—is one of the most distressing aspects of the quarterlife crisis, particularly for individuals who do not have large support networks or who doubt themselves often. It is in these situations that the quarterlife crisis becomes not just a common stage—it can become hazardous. Not everyone at the age of the quarterlife encounters some sort of depression. . . . But we are addressing depression as one common result of the quarterlife crisis here so that we can illustrate why it is so important to acknowledge this transition period.

After interviewing dozens of twentysomethings who said they were depressed because of the transition, we ran our conclusions by Robert DuPont, a Georgetown Medical School professor of psychology who wrote *The Anxiety Cure*. "Based on my experience," DuPont said, "I have found that there is a high rate of all forms of disorder in this age group, including addiction, anxiety, depression, and many other kinds of problems because of the high stress associated with the transition from being a child to being an adult. And that has gotten more stressful as the road map has become less used. The old way of doing this was to get out and get it done right away. There was an economic imperative to doing it. It's not like that anymore. And as the road map has disappeared, the stress has gone up. People have to invent their own road map. It used to be that it came with the college graduation. Now you have to go out and figure it out yourself."

These high rates of disorders, however, have gone virtually unacknowledged. That's why we can't bog you down with statistics on this age group. They don't exist. Psychological research on twentysomethings, including statistics on depression and suicide, has not been performed. We asked major national mental health associations such as the National Institutes of Mental Health, the American Psychiatric Association, and the National Depressive and Manic Depressive Association for any information they had on people in their twenties. They didn't have any. As one psychologist told us, associations don't cut the data to incorporate this age group. "It's not a subject that's interesting to them. They just lump everybody together," he said. . . .

Another way the quarterlife crisis can show up, particularly in the mid- to late twenties, is in a feeling of disappointment, of "This is all there is?" Maybe the job turns out to be not so glamorous after all, or maybe it just doesn't seem to lead anywhere interesting. Perhaps the year of travel in Europe was more of a wallet buster than previously imagined—even with nights in youth hostels and meals of ramen. Or maybe the move to a hip, new city just didn't turn out to be as fabulous a relocation as expected.

While these are, according to older generations, supposed to be the best years of their lives, twentysomethings also feel that the choices they make during this period will influence their thirties, forties, fifties, and on, in an irreparable domino effect. As a result, twentysomethings frequently have the unshakable belief that this is the time during which they have to nail down the meaning in their lives, which explains why they often experience a nagging feeling that somehow they need to make their lives more fulfilling.

This is why there are so many drastic life changes at this point in life: an investment banker breaks off his engagement and volunteers for the Peace Corps; a consultant suddenly frets that consulting may not really have that much influence on other people's lives; a waiter chucks the steady paycheck to live in his car and try to make it in Hollywood; a law school graduate decides she doesn't want to be a lawyer after all and seeks a job in technology.

The changes hurtling toward a young adult, as well as the potential for more changes ahead, can be excruciatingly overwhelming for someone who is trying so hard to figure out how to feel fulfilled. A lot of people don't realize just how suffocating this pressure can be. The prevalent belief is that twentysomethings have it relatively easy because they do not have as many responsibilities as older individuals. But it is precisely this reduced responsibility that renders the vast array of decisions more difficult to make. For instance, if there were, say, a family to consider, a mother might not be as inclined to take a risk on the stock market. If a guy's elderly father were sick, he probably wouldn't take that year off to travel in South America. Twentysomethings, for the most part, just aren't at those stages yet, which is why they are sometimes envied. But because their choices aren't narrowed down for them by responsibilities, they have more decisions to make. And while this isn't necessarily bad, it can make things pretty complex. Figuring out which changes to make in order to make life more fulfilling is hard enough. But deciding to make a change and then following through with it requires an extraordinary amount of strength, which is sometimes hard to come by for a recent graduate who has not had to rely solely on himself for very long.

The most widespread, frightening, and quite possibly the most difficult manifestation of the quarterlife crisis is a feeling that can creep up on a twenty something whether he is unemployed, living at home, and friendless, or in an interesting job, with a great apartment, and dozens of buddies. Regardless of their levels of self-esteem, confidence, and overall well-being, twentysomethings are particularly vulnerable to doubts. They doubt their decisions, their abilities, their readiness, their past, present, and future . . . but most of all, they doubt themselves. The twenties comprise a period of intense questioning—of introspection and self-development that young adults often feel they are not ready for. The questions can range from seemingly trivial choices—"Should I really have spent $100 to join that fantasy baseball league?"—to irrefutably mammoth decisions—"When is the right time for me to start a family?" It is healthy, of course, for people to question themselves some; an occasional self-assessment or life inventory is a natural part of the quest for improvement. But if the questioning becomes constant and the barrage of doubts never seems to cease, twentysomethings can feel as if it is hard to catch their breath, as if they are spiraling downward. Many times the doubts increase because twentysomethings think it is abnormal to have them in the first place. No one talks about having doubts at this age, so when twentysomethings do find that they are continuously questioning themselves, they think something is wrong with them.

Questions for Writing and Discussion

1. Robbins and Wilner describe the quarterlife crisis as something that occurs because of "too many choices" during a time when life is "supposed to be 'easy.'" Write about a time in your life when you felt you had too many choices, or that life was supposed to be easy, but wasn't. How did you handle this situation? What did you learn from it?

2. In paragraph 6, the authors talk about the structure and goal-oriented path of education. Do you see your educational path in the same way? Why or why not?

3. One reason twentysomethings experience this crisis, according to Robbins and Wilner, is that they are disappointed with their lives after college. What are your expectations for life after college? How realistic do you think these expectations are? What will you have to do to ensure that your expectations become reality?

4. Besides a midlife or quarterlife crisis, describe a point in your life, or the lives of others you know, that required decision making based on unexpected realities. Do you think that experiencing this, or witnessing it in others, will better prepare you for the future? Why or why not?

Making Connections

1. Robbins and Wilner ("What Is the Quarterlife Crisis?") and Klass ("Ambition") touch on the causes and effects of disappointment. Describe a situation in which you confronted disappointment. What did you learn? If your experience relates to what the authors from these selections discuss, draw some comparisons.

2. In "The Nontraditional Student in You," Michele Compton and Candy Schock touch on a number of issues relevant to nontraditional students that have been brought up in earlier selections, including Erin Mallants Rodriguez's "Universities Seeing a Gender Gap in Enrollments" (Chapter Two), Danielle Barbuto's "From Single Mom to Successful Student" (Chapter Three), and Malcolm X's "Saved" (Chapter Three). Choose a topic that one of these selections shares with Compton and Schock's piece and compare their point of view with that of the other author.

3. What does it mean to be an educated person? Consider your own definition using both evidence from the readings you've done in this book as well as examples from your experience and other sources. Once you have defined this term, consider whether you see yourself as an educated person. If so, why? If not, how will you become one?

Exploring the Web

Education Index: Liberal Arts and Sciences Resources

http://www.educationindex.com/liberal/
This portion of Education Index, a site sponsored by Hobsons, an international college and career publisher, provides a number of links to online documents posted mainly by members of college communities who provide a variety of perspectives on liberal arts education.

Association of Nontraditional Students in Higher Education

http://antshe.org/
"Association of Nontraditional Students in Higher Education (ANTSHE) is an international partnership of students, academic professionals, institutions and organizations whose mission is to encourage and coordinate support, education and advocacy for the adult learning community." This site includes a number of resources for nontraditional students across the world, including listservs, links, and scholarship opportunities.

Wikipedia

http://www.wikipedia.com
Wikipedia is on online collaborative encyclopedia authored "by people all over the world." "Anyone with access to an Internet-connected computer" may write or edit an entry on Wikipedia. According to Wikipedia.com, Wikipedia is "the largest reference Web site on the Internet."

CREDITS

CHAPTER 1

Lubrano, Alfred, "Bricklayer's Boy." First appeared in *Gentlemen's Quarterly*. Reprinted by permission of the author.

Oliphant, Thomas, "Abandoned, But Not Alone." First appeared in *The Boston Globe*. Reprinted by permission of the Boston Globe Company.

Rodriguez, Rodrigo Joseph, "The Meaning of Work." Reprinted by permission of the author. Originally published in *Hispanic Magazine* (October 1999). Reprinted from *Kenyon College Alumni Bulletin*, vol. 22, no. 1 (Spring 2000).

Suina, Joseph H., "And Then I Went to School." From *Linguistic and Cultural Influences on Learning Mathematics* by Joseph H. Suina. Reprinted by permission of the author and Lawrence Erlbaum Associates, Inc.

Suskind, Ron, "Let the Colors Run." From *A Hope in the Unseen* by Ron Suskind, copyright© 1998 by Ron Suskind. Used by permission of Broadway Books, a division of Random House, Inc.

Tan, Amy, "Mother Tongue." Copyright © 1990 by Amy Tan. First appeared in *The Threepenny Review*. Reprinted by permission of the author and the Sandra Dijkstra Literary Agency.

CHAPTER 2

Daum, Meghan, "We're Lying: Safe Sex and White Lies in the Time of AIDS" by Meghan Daum, 1995. First appeared in the *New York Times Magazine*. Reprinted by permission of International Creative Management, Inc.

Dince, Rebecca, "Could Your Facebook Profile Throw a Wrench in Your Future?" Copyright © 2006 by Rebecca Dince. First appeared in the *Tufts Daily*. Reprinted with permission of the author.

Kramer, Martin, "Earning and Learning: Are Students Working Too Much?" First Appeared in *Change*, vol. 26 (1994): 6. Reprinted with permission of Helen Dwight Reid Educational Foundation. Published by Heldref Publications, 1319 Eighteenth St., NW, Washington, DC 20036-1802. Copyright © 1994.

Mallants Rodriguez, Erin, "Universities Seeing a Gender Gap in Enrollments" by Erin Mallants Rodriguez, 2005. First appeared Miami Herald Online. Reprinted by permission of Miami Herald.

Sink, Mindy, "Drinking Deaths Draw Attention to Old Campus Problem." Copyright © 2004 by the New York Times Co. Reprinted with permission.

Tesich, Steve, "Focusing on Friends" by Steve Tesich, 1983. Reprinted by permission of International Creative Management, Inc.

CHAPTER 3

Barbuto, Danielle, "From Single Mother to Successful Student." Reprinted by permission of the author.

Finkel, Ed, "Sticky Fingers on the Information Superhighway." First appeared in *Community College Week* (February 28, 2005). Reprinted by permission.

Gardner, Howard, "Multiple Intelligences." Copyright © 1993 by Howard Gardner. Reprinted by permission of Basic Books, a member of Perseus Books, LLC.

Gilbert, Julie, "ADHD: The Cloud Lifted." Reprinted by permission of the author.

Graham, Paul, "Good and Bad Procrastination." From www.paulgraham.com. Copyright © 2005. Reprinted by permission of the author.

Morse, Jodi, "Log On To Learn." First appeared in *Time Digital: Supplement to TIME Magazine* (December 2000). Reprinted by Time, Inc.

"Saved" copyright © 1964 by Alex Haley and Malcolm X. Copyright © 1965 by Alex Haley and Betty Shabbaz. From *The Autobiography of Malcolm X* by Malcolm X and Alex Haley. Used by permission of Random House, Inc.

CHAPTER 4

Nafisi, Azar, "Upsilamda." From *Reading Lolita in Tehran* by Azar Nafisi. Copyright © 2002 by Azar Nafisi. Used by permission of Random House, Inc.

Roberts, Paul, "How to Say Nothing in Five Hundred Words." From *Understanding English* by Paul Roberts. Copyright© 1958 by Paul Roberts. Reprinted by permission of Pearson Education, Inc.

Robinson, Adam, "Take This Quiz." From *What Smart Students Know: Maximum Grades, Optimum Learning* by Adam Robinson. Copyright © 1993 by Adam Robinson. Used by permission of Crown Publishers, a division of Random House.

Rose, Mike, "I Just Wanna Be Average." Reprinted with the permission of The Free Press, a Division of Simon and Schuster, Inc., from *Lives on the Boundary: The Struggles and Achievements of America's Underprepared* by Mike Rose. Copyright © 1989 by Mike Rose.

Tobias, Shelia, "Symptoms of Math Anxiety." From *Overcoming Math Anxiety, Revised and Expanded Edition* by Sheila Tobias. Copyright © 1993, 1978 by Sheila Tobias. Used by permission of W. W. Norton & Company, Inc.

CHAPTER 5

Compton, Michele, and Candy Schock, "The Non-Traditional Student in You." First appeared in *Women in Business*, vol. 54, no. 4 (2000): 14–16. Reprinted by permission of the authors.